Irene Neddie Muyambi,

the Virtuous Woman

Irene Neddie Muyambi,

the Virtuous Woman

An Inspiring True Story of a Wife of a Priest. Buried in a
Private Chapel. The Aftermath of Her Departure

Tsitsi Dorcas Jongwe

To order additional copies of this book, contact:
Xlibris
800-056-3182
www.Xlibrispublishing.co.uk
Orders@Xlibrispublishing.co.uk
767217

Contents

Foreword

Throughout history, women have been crucial to the growth and flourishing of the church. The lives they touch, the generosity they share, and the care they give becomes their spiritual legacy for those who come after they depart from this world. One of our Church of England most recognised and best-loved spiritual leaders, Mother Irene Neddie Muyambi, inspired thousands with her extraordinary example of compassionate and selfless work for the poor, the ill, and the outcast. Irene had a steadfast voice of love and faith, providing immeasurable kindness and guidance to the world's down trodden.

Irene was a woman who humbled herself right up to the time of her death. Whilst on her hospital bed and in excruciating pain, she asked for some water, but the doctor's instructions were clear in the mind of those who were with her: "No water." Her request might have been denied by the doctors, but the Lord heard her cry and called her to the ever-flowing spring of life and to a completed mansion where there is no more pain and no more suffering. Irene's journey here on earth had come to an end, and her new life had just begun. The holy angels were waiting for her, and the table had been set for her heavenly banquet.

It is great honour for me to be asked to write this foreword, because although Irene's spiritual journey is the story of her life, her experience and legacy will speak to many. It is my hope that as you read this book, you will examine yourself and learn from Irene's humility, integrity, kindness, generosity, and above all, love for her God and all around her.

"Later, knowing that all was now completed, and so that the Scripture would be fulfilled, Jesus said, 'I am thirsty'" (John 19:28).
May Irene's soul rest in peace eternally.

Reverend Canon Lameck Mutete

Foreword

In November 2016, I received a frantic telephone call from my church warden, who wanted to come and speak to me as soon as possible. Ten minutes later we were sitting together, and he explained the dilemma that his wife was experiencing. She was stuck in Zimbabwe, having lost her travel documents to robbers. (See Tinaye Matsveru's story, "Strange Incident at Funeral Gathering in Harare: Handbag Disappears", within these pages.)

Godsen Jongwe, very upset, couldn't imagine how the situation could be resolved. To cut a long story short, his wife, Tsitsi Dorcas, had made an emergency trip home to Zimbabwe to be with her mother, who had become dangerously ill. In the time it took to arrange the flights and get to Zimbabwe, her mother, Irene Neddie Muyambi, sadly had died.

Tsitsi Dorcas's arrival in Zimbabwe was far from smooth. Sometime during the first night she was there, her handbag containing all of her travel documents was stolen. Her passport, her visa, her phone, and everything else her handbag could contain was gone.

Mr Jongwe and I talked and prayed. Throughout our time together, I had a strong sense that this unplanned detention in Zimbabwe was for a purpose.

Over the following days, we worked with our MP and others to begin to gather the documents necessary for Tsitsi Dorcas to return to England.

The purpose for her detainment is now clear. It was to support her elderly father, Reverend Lazarus Muyambi, who in his ninth decade continues to work at Gokwe, to pray for the sick, and to father the orphans and the homeless. The other purpose of Tsitsi Dorcas's stay in Zimbabwe, which is now clear, was to write this story of her mother's amazing and faith-filled life.

I first met Tsitsi Dorcas, her husband, and their two younger children in 2007. I had been asked to visit their new home and to bless it. My theology is such that I don't bless things (not even houses), but I do bless people—and that is how our friendship began. Since that time, I have met all of Tsitsi Dorcas's siblings who live in the West, and I continue to support her father and his work in Gokwe.

I continue to be challenged by their faith, by their stories of healing, and by the ways in which they have been a blessing to our small church community and have been blessed themselves, through God's provision. In the West, many of us have become complacent and rarely look to God for healing, when a tablet or a trip to the doctor will do the trick. In Africa and in so many other parts of the world, it is not so easy to get required medication, so vibrant faith and the witnessing of miracles is more common place.

I did not meet Tsitsi Dorcas's amazing mother, but her life of looking after sick people, orphans, and disadvantaged people speaks volumes about her nature and about from where her satisfaction in life was derived. And her fifty-seven years of marriage to a man who was battling with evil spirits and people's illnesses is not something to be taken lightly. Housing orphans and welcoming every stranger who passed by her doorstep and giving them food or drink, Irene appears to have been a true supporter of her husband and was determined never to see his ministry die down. This is evidence of a true partnership in the gospel, the actions and the dedication of their lives. It's very clear that Irene lived to see her dream fulfilled, bringing up her own children in the path of faith, as evidenced by what we see in her children.

It is my prayer that by reading this book, others will be challenged as I have when it comes to their faith and the power of God to heal in 2018.

Reverend Susan K. Barter

Preface

The Wife of Noble Character

A wife of noble character who can find?

She is worth far more than rubies. Her husband has full confidence in her and lacks nothing of value. She brings him good, not harm, all the days of her life. She selects wool and flax and works with eager hands. She is like the merchant ships, bringing her food from afar. She gets up while it is still night; she provides food for her family and portions for her female servants. She considers a field and buys it; out of her earnings she plants a vineyard. She sets about her work vigorously; her arms are strong for her tasks. She sees that her trading is profitable, and her lamp does not go out at night.

In her hand she holds the distaff and grasps the spindle with her fingers. She opens her arms to the poor and extends her hands to the needy. When it snows, she has no fear for her household; for all of them are clothed in scarlet. She makes coverings for her bed; she is clothed in fine linen and purple. Her husband is respected at the city gate, where he takes his seat among the elders of the land.

She makes linen garments and sells them, and supplies the merchants with sashes. She is clothed with strength and dignity; she can laugh at the days to come.

She speaks with wisdom, and faithful instruction is on her tongue. She watches over the affairs of her household and does not eat the bread of idleness. Her children arise and call her blessed; her husband also, and he praises her: "Many women do noble things, but you surpass them all."

Charm is deceptive, and beauty is fleeting; but a woman who fears the Lord is to be praised. Honor her for all that her hands have done, and let her works bring her praise at the city gate.

(Proverbs 31)

Acknowledgements

I would like to say thank you to everyone who helped me to make this book a success. Thanks to all the people mentioned in this book whom I approached and asked to give me information about the life that they experienced with Irene Neddie. My greatest appreciation goes to Chipo Baira, Sister Phoebe, Sister Lilian, Rodha Madovi and my daughter Doctor Careen Jongwe-Muriva, all of whom gave me information about Neddie's last moments on earth.

Thanks to Reverend Canon Lazarus Muyambi for the long hours of sitting and giving me information about the life of Neddie. What a loss it is to him. How is he going to cope without her? My greatest appreciation also goes to everyone I spoke to as I gathered more information about Neddie's life.

Many thanks to my husband, Godsen Jongwe; my brothers, Anesu and Izwi Muyambi; and my daughter Redemption Zvikomborero Jongwe, a film production graduate of the University of Worcester, for the support they gave me to complete this book.

• • • • • • • • ● • • • • • • • • •

Introduction

This book was written soon after the death of a woman widely known for looking after orphans, the sick, and the suffering, a woman whose faith was beyond measure. Irene Neddie Muyambi was well known for her peacefulness, her forgiving nature, and her resemblance to the wife described in Proverbs 31. She stood by her husband in providing shelter for the sick, orphans and abandoned people of society.

I spoke to many people about her and listened to graveside speeches. If the Church of England really considered people like her to be important, she would have been given a better honour than the burial she was awarded. Her body rests in the private chapel built by her and her husband. Neddie will be remembered by all who appreciate great works, especially those done by a woman. Thousands of people who passed through her hands received assistance in one way or another. Her great deeds will forever live. She was the wife of a priest/vicar, a former teacher, a headmistress, a counsellor, and a comforter. This book seeks to make readers understand why Neddie's life and death touched and impacted the lives of so many who crossed her path.

PART I

Biography

Irene Neddie was born 14 April 1941. She was the eldest of the four children of Edward and Sophia Mashinya. Neddie was the last surviving member of her family upon her death on 21 November 2016, at 2.30 p.m., in Avenues Clinic in Harare, Zimbabwe. She will be greatly missed by those whose lives she touched.

Further information about Neddie is included in her husband's narrative of the life he shared with her.

The Illness and Death of Irene Neddie Muyambi

Irene Neddie fell ill on Sunday, 20 November 2016. It is said that on her walk to church that Sunday morning, she made three stops to sit and rest before arriving at church, which was unlike her. Once at church, she sat in the back. However, after the sermon, she made her way up to the front of the church to sit in her usual place. Observers said she wasn't her usual self, sitting on the bench with her head down. Neddie was prompted to go and receive Holy Communion by Mrs Mazula, the wife of the acting priest in charge. After church, Neddie slowly walked home, stopping four times. One of the orphans whom Neddie had cared for, Chipo Baira, came and assisted her home.

Chipo's Narrative

It was on Sunday, 20 November 2016, when Mother came into church during the sermon. I was surprised because this was the first time I had seen her arrive late to church. Curious about why this had happened, I kept my eye on her as I sat by the altar. She sat at the back of the church, which was unlike her. After the sermon, Mother walked to the front of the church and took her usual place where priests' wives sit. I noticed she wasn't singing. Instead, she just nodded her head and appeared very sleepy.

After church, I remained to finish my serving duties in the vestry room. Afterwards, I walked to the orphanage and caught up with Mother. She had sat down to rest outside the orphanage. When I greeted her, she responded in a way that made it evident to me that she was not feeling well. After she spoke to Sencia Rodha Madovi, who works for the Logos High School and resides at the orphanage, she stood to walk, but then she staggered, as if about to fall. I assumed she was dizzy. I quickly grabbed her by her elbow and linked our arms to support her. This stopped her from falling. We slowly walked to her home.

I asked Mum if she had come to church by car. She said she had walked because Sister Phoebe was tending to Mum's husband, Lazarus, who was very unwell. When I asked to phone Sister Phoebe to see if she could drive Mum home, Mum said that Sister Phoebe was not able to leave Lazarus because of his condition. Mum worried more about her husband than about herself. Mum appeared very tired. Her breathing was audible; I had never heard her breathe this way before. She said her legs and shoulders were in pain. Mum rested by a pole near the orphanage and then again by the pump house.

I asked her why her breathing was so loud and laboured, but she indicated she was not aware of it. I asked her if she had gone to the hospital. She informed me that she had gone to Partners Surgery.

Neddie leaned against a pole by the Tashaya residence before walking through the gate to her homestead. She again told me her shoulders and legs hurt. When we got to the homestead, she asked me to wait so she could give me freezits to sell. I left her at her home and went back to the orphanage.

Comment

From Chipo's narrative, it is clear that Neddie was unwell and needed urgent medical attention. It appears she was more concerned about her eighty-two-year-old husband's health than her own health.

This girl, Chipo, was very kind when Neddie needed help. An adult would have noticed that Neddie needed medical attention.

Neddie's Seven Stations before Death

According to Chipo, Neddie stopped at the orphanage and took some rest. She stopped by a fence pole on the side of the orphanage farthest away from the church. She stopped by the pump house. Then she stopped again by the fence pole near to her house. The next stations were her house, Gokwe Hospital, and finally Harare Avenues Clinic.

When Chipo left Neddie at the Muyambi residence, what transpired next? Sister Phoebe and Lazarus were at home and watched the events as they unfolded.

Sister Phoebe is a nun at the Convent of the Community of the Gifts of the Holy Fire (CZM) and a former arch-sister. Neddie had asked her to move into the Muyambi residence so that she could assist with the care of Neddie's husband, Lazarus. Following is how Sister Phoebe interpreted the events.

Sister Phoebe's Narrative

Neddie woke up on Friday, 18 November 2016, saying she had not slept well and that her back and legs were in pain. She said she wanted to rest and was not going to the preschool, where she was the manager. She asked to be left alone to rest in the spare bedroom at the back of her house. Neddie asked me to give her milk and water so that she could spend the day drinking without disturbance.

On Saturday, 19 November 2016, Neddie woke up saying she had slept well. But when I looked her over, she appeared weak. On this day, there was going to be a function at the newly built clinic to officially inform invited delegates it was open. Neddie came to this event, and we celebrated together.

Saturday night, we stayed awake until late, sitting in the lounge. Neddie asked Lazarus how far the issue of their title deed had gotten. They briefly discussed the subject, and then they prayed about it. These title deeds were for the stands they had acquired from Gokwe city council, they had built shelters over the years and now they needed full ownership by having their title deeds. After prayer, Lazarus went to bed. I remained with Mum, chatting. Neddie said to me, "Sister Phoebe, look after Lazarus as the founder of the Convent of the Community of the Gifts of the Holy Fire. I have taught you how to do this work, so carry on." I asked Neddie why she was saying this. In response, she said, "Make cups of tea for us to drink. Death came into the world." We drank tea and chatted. Lazarus heard us and asked us to go to bed.

On Sunday, 20 November 2016, Neddie said she had not slept well. She said she would have a cup of tea and eat porridge later.

She asked me to check her sugar and blood pressure, together with Lazarus's. I did that before going to the 6.30 a.m. secondary-school students' Sunday morning Mass at the Healing Centre, Trinity Chapel. Lazarus joined me in going to the service, but as we approached the chapel, he said that his body was getting weak. He sat in the vestry room with his head down on the table. I went back home. Neddie had already eaten her porridge and taken her medication. She gave me Lazarus's porridge and medication, and asked me to rush back to Lazarus. I promised to come and take her to church as usual by car.

On returning from church with Lazarus, I found that Neddie had locked the doors and gone to church. She had put ingredients for breakfast on the table. I cooked and served Lazarus his breakfast.

I then saw Neddie coming into the dining room and giving freezits to Chipo (the girl who had walked Neddie home after church) to sell. Neddie came into the sitting room, where Lazarus and I were seated. What bothered me was the way she threw herself onto the sofa. I gave her food, which she gratefully accepted. She washed her hands and ate. But she did not eat in her usual way. She started coughing continuously. After the cough, she did not carry on eating. I tested her blood sugar. It was high, at 14.8. Her blood pressure was 90/50. I realised Neddie was not feeling well at all. I called Lazarus, and he came and prayed for her. He gave her five hundred millilitres of holy water to drink. The weather was very hot. Neddie's right hand was so weak that she could not hold a glass.

We took Neddie outside, where there was open space and fresh air. Lazarus instructed me to phone Mrs Muteto and ask for advice. She advised that we put two tablespoons of sugar and a quarter teaspoon of salt in a glass of water. Mrs Muteto said that after taking the solution, Neddie should lie in a recovery position. This is a position in which one lies on their side allowing any secretions from the mouth or nose to escape without chocking the patient. We did that, and she lay down for about thirty minutes.

Neddie awoke, crying and saying she was in great pain. Sister Eugenia, a qualified nurse based in New Zealand, came from the Community of Holy Fire (CZM) and did what she could. Neddie's children phoned from the United Kingdom and Australia and requested that Neddie be taken to hospital immediately.

**Irene and Sister Phoebe CZM receiving
donations for the orphans**

Gokwe Hospital

We all accompanied Neddie to Gokwe General Hospital. Reverend and Mrs Mazula came to the hospital too. There was no medication at the hospital and no electricity. Neddie was later given a furosemide injection which we had purchased, but it did not stop the pain. She slept for only five minutes. She spent the whole night in hospital receiving no help. Crying out in pain, she was so restless that it was pathetic. Her children were phoning and speaking to her, but because of her pain, the conversations were difficult. Neddie's grandchild, Doctor Careen, sent an ambulance, which took longer than expected. It arrived at 6 a.m. on Monday, 21 November 2016. Sister Lilian from the Convent of the Community of the Gifts of the Holy Fire accompanied Neddie in the ambulance to Harare.

Comment

Analysing the foregoing narrative of Sister Phoebe, it is clear to me that Neddie worried a great deal about the title deeds of the projects she had worked so hard on during her life of selflessness and dedication to serving people and God. The reason why Neddie and Lazarus were not being given their title deeds was a mystery. Neddie was a teacher. Whenever donations were not forthcoming, she and Lazarus put their personal money into the work, as their joy came from the completion of each project. They also begged for money from their friends, well wishers and family. They had started out with no van to transport school children to and from trips, but eventually they had a fleet of vans.

On this particular Sunday, Neddie suffered a great deal of pain for a long period without being given proper attention. The sister in charge at the hospital was informed that the ambulance was no longer coming from Kwekwe, the nearest city, but instead would be coming from Harare, some three hundred kilometres away. They waited endlessly for an ambulance that was meant to arrive in two hours but that arrived 6 a.m. the following day. Was Neddie really meant to suffer this excruciating pain all night and day? The ambulance sent was not the proper type for people with acute conditions. Neddie's medical aid policy included the benefit of air rescue, which if taken advantage of in this case could have made a huge difference in terms of the timescale. Attention was not given to the urgency of the matter. She died the same way people who drown do: struggling for breath. Another cause of death were the ailments in her body, as explained at post mortem.

The suffering that Neddie went through up to her last minute reminds me of the suffering our Lord Jesus Christ endured at the hands of his tormentors. All night and morning he was tortured, until they hung him on the cross and until he put his Spirit into God's hands. After doing so much good on earth, did Jesus have to suffer? After doing so much good on earth, did Neddie deserve such torment, torture, and suffering for a good twenty-four hours? Everything that happened really tormented her, including the ailments in her body. God allowed this to happen in the same way that he allowed Jesus to go through suffering for the sake of the world. In the same way, he allowed Job to suffer physically. Like a sheep led to its slaughter, Neddie silently succumbed to her death.

Let us hear from Sister Lilian about how she journeyed with Neddie in an ambulance to Harare.

Sister Lilian's (CZM) Journey with Neddie to Harare

Sister Lilian is a nun at the Convent of the Community of the Gifts of the Holy Fire (CZM). She works at Logos Girls' Secondary School. The following are her words.

On Monday, 21 November 2016, we left Gokwe Hospital in an ambulance just after 6 a.m. Neddie was in agony. She was saying her whole body was sore. She was injected with another painkiller, but it did not help. All the way, Neddie complained of pain. I comforted her and reassured her that once we got to Harare, she would be fine, as she would be under the care of specialist doctors. She was restless and breathless. Neddie was put on oxygen.

As we approached Zimbabwe's capital city, Harare, Neddie asked if we had not reached Harare yet, saying again that she was in great pain. I informed her that we were nearer to the hospital. She asked for water, and I gave her some. I tried to sing one of her favourite songs:

> Vatsvene vepasi navo
> Vatsvene vakafa,
> Ngavaimbe pamwe navo,
> Varanda vaKristu.

Avenues Clinic in Harare

When we got to the hospital, Neddie was quickly attended to and given a bed. Doctors tried to get a vein to inject furosemide into her and drain fluids from her body, but they could not find one because her whole body was swollen. She had had two drips (intravenous fluids) administered at Gokwe. Her feet and hands were already cold. She was finally injected via a vein in her neck. The doctor instructed that Neddie should not be given water. Neddie asked for water, which we could not give her. She asked why we were denying her water when she was so thirsty.

Comment

From Sister Lilian's narrative, it is plain that Neddie was in a hot oven of torment as she faced the cross of Jesus and journeyed through her last moments on earth. Her whole body was in anguish. As our Lord Jesus Christ asked for water while hanging on the cross, so did Neddie ask, as she was in anguish. Commentaries say that Jesus's thirst was not for water but to do God's work. One would wonder what Neddie's thirst was for. Probably to carry on preaching the Word of God or to carry on building for the needy. Maybe she was thirsting to get her title deeds, which she was being denied. Maybe she was thirsting to look after her husband until death did them part. We don't know what Neddie's thirst was about as the intravenous fluids ran through her body. She could have been thirsting to sing for God, seeing as she was gifted in that, and had done it all her life. Maybe she was thirsting for the CZM to be united under their founder, Lazarus or to preach the gospel of salvation, or for Mothers' Union's objectives to support families to be adhered to, or to see her children who were abroad. The list could go on. As far as Neddie was known, her passion was to read the Bible, fast, pray, preach, sing, receive visitors and help the needy from all walks of life. She had applied for land on which to build a boys' high school and a university.

As her favourite song was sung by Sister Lilian, what could have been in her mind? Her grandmother had lived for one hundred years. Her mum had lived for ninety-two years. No one was looking forward to Neddie's departure from this world so soon. She left behind her husband, Lazarus, their six biological children, one adopted child, grandchildren and numerous orphans all over the world whom she had raised under her roof and in the orphanage. She left all the projects she had tirelessly worked for in Gokwe and all their employees.

Neddie and her husband are the founders and owners of the following organisations:

- the Healing Centre
- the Healing and Medical Clinic
- the CZM Primary School
- the St Agnes Children's Home and Preschool
- the Convent of the Community of the Gifts of the Holy Fire
- the monastery of friars
- Logos Girls' Secondary School
- the CZM Taderera primary school.

Neddie left the Loving and Caring Members (LCM) who support the above projects. They wear crosses on a red string, symbolising the suffering of Jesus and the holy fire/Holy Spirit. Neddie left all the members of the Mothers' Union, a charitable organisation within the Church of England, which is a pillar of that institution. She was a member of this organisation for fifty-seven years, counselling individuals and couples who were either getting married or on the verge of divorcing.

Neddie left the St Agnes Guild, made up of young girls whom she had prepared for marriage and for sisterhood. She left the St Agnes Mission congregation, which she had worked with since 1972. It was tremendously sad. The whole village was in agony. Sister Phoebe was hospitalised after failing to come into terms with the death of Irene Neddie.

It was a loss. Gokwe had lost a mother. Gokwe town, banks, and shops; the Gokwe Hospital; the government offices; and the education sector from the district level to the provincial level all lost a dear mother who loved everyone irrespective of their background. Neddie was a hard worker, a comforter, and a peacemaker.

Neddie's grandchild Doctor Careen was in Harare waiting for the arrival of her grandmother. She had run around to make sure all the paperwork for her mother's CIMAS medical aid was up to date so the latter could be attended to. Dr Careen also made sure specialist doctors were ready at the Avenues Clinic to receive Neddie. Dr Careen sat at Avenues Clinic waiting for Neddie, who took a very long time to arrive because the ambulance service was not efficient in this time of need.

Doctor Careen Welcomes Her Ailing Grandmother in Harare

Grandma, you were my hardest goodbye.

Dr Careen Fungai Muriva

I was waiting for my granny at Avenues Clinic, having processed all her paperwork for admission and contacted a specialist physician. I kept pacing up and down the reception area as the ambulance seemed to take forever to arrive. The receptionist advised me to sit down, saying she would notify me as soon as the ambulance arrived. Being too anxious, I ignored her instruction and went outside to the ambulance drive-in area. There I was told the ambulance had just arrived but that Granny's bags were still inside it. I raced upstairs and found Sister Lilian waiting for admission. I informed the nurses that I was a doctor. I got to Grandma's bed and had the shock of my life. The condition she was in is simply unexplainable. She was in pain, panting, and grunting desperately for every breath. Grandma was transferred to the hospital bed. I stood at her bedside, held her hand, and informed her I was there. She said, "Thank you for coming."

I noticed the drip on her. I immediately stopped it and asked the ambulance staff who had given the order for the drip to be put on. I got no answer. I immediately called the specialist physician and asked her to come at once, adding that Grandma's condition was bad. She was on oxygen delivered through nasal prongs, which she kept removing, so we asked for a face mask to be put instead. I called my husband and my uncle Tapiwa to come immediately. My mum, Tsitsi Dorcas, phoned from the United Kingdom. Because of the fear, emotion, and anxiety that was overwhelming me, I moved to a different ward to talk to her. I broke down in tears as I tried to explain to Mum that Grandma's condition was not as stable as we had thought. Mum told me to be strong and to do the best I could. After regaining my composure, I went back to Grandma.

The physician arrived, examined Grandma, and informed us that her lungs were flooded, which made it impossible for the physician to properly hear her heart sounds. The physician tried to insert a cannula, but because Grandma's body was swollen all over, it was very difficult to find a vein. My husband eventually secured one on the side of her neck. Furosemide was administered to drain the fluid from my grandmother's body. An ICU bed was ordered, and an anaesthetist was called to come and oversee the transfer to the ICU. As we waited for him, Sister Lilian and I stood by Grandma's bed, trying to restrain her. Grandma kept on saying "Let me go" and trying to get off the bed.

Grandma was not saying much, but at one point she looked at me and said, "*Fungie, ita basa rako*" (Fungie, do your job). These words cut me through to the core of my heart. She started saying, "*Ndaneta. Ndipeiwo mvura?*" (I am tired. Can I have some water?) We could not give her the water because the specialist doctor had instructed us to refrain from giving her fluids.

The anaesthetist arrived, examined Grandma, and literally ran to the ICU to start the preparations for Neddie. He said her condition was critical. As we were about to leave, Grandma leaned over onto my chest. I put my arms around her and held her. I tried to explain to her that we were going to the ICU, where she was to receive further help. At that point I was optimistic. I and Sister Lilian followed behind, with the physician and other nurses pushing Grandma's bed hurriedly to an elevator to take us to the ICU on the third floor.

We got to the ICU. As we were trying to push Grandma's bed into one of the rooms, I noticed that her pattern of breathing had changed. I shook her and shouted, *"Mbuya"* (Grandma). She sighed once and collapsed once onto her bed. I shook her again, but this time she did not respond.

I was restrained and prevented from entering the ICU room. Immediately a crash trolley was called for. It was at this moment that I realised Grandma could possibly die, a thought that had not previously crossed my mind despite her dire condition. In tears, I was led to sit outside in the corridor. I phoned my grandmother's eldest son, Uncle Anesu, in the United Kingdom to inform him that Grandma was being resuscitated. I also informed my husband Doctor Muriva, my uncle Tapiwa, and my aunt Mrs Nhepera. After I'd waited for over thirty minutes (Grandma was confirmed dead at 2.30 p.m.), the doctors came. I could tell from the way they were avoiding eye contact that they were not bearing good news. They asked my husband, my uncle Tapiwa and his fiancé Patience and Sister Lilian to sit in a nearby office. I ran to my grandma. My husband followed. There she lay, motionless. I shook her, calling out desperately, "Mbuya! Mbuya! Mbuya!", hoping she could make a movement. I lay on her chest crying in defeat as my husband tried to console me. Mbuya was gone. My one and only friend was gone, the woman I communicated with more than any other relative.

Grandma had taken the place of my mum since my mum lived in the UK. If it came to pass that I didn't call my grandmother for some time, she would text me to say, *"Kunyarara kwako idambudziko remwoyo wangu,"* which meant that my silence bothered her. She had called me two days before she fell ill, telling me about Edwin Munyoro's death (see *Christian Healing Mission in Gokwe, Zimbabwe: A Success Story*) and saying, *"Honawo muendero unoita vamwe"* (See how other people die), as if she knew she was going to die a painful death. I thought this was a weird phone call, with Mbuya telling me about someone I did not know. She sounded so lively and jovial during the conversation that I did not put much thought into it. If only I had known.

Comment

From Doctor Careen's narrative, it is clear that Neddie was distraught, ragged, and destroyed by this pain. Having family around was reassuring, but for how long? Neddie had asked Dr Careen to do her job. Here she could have meant that Careen should help her alleviate this pain. She could have meant to be giving a word of advice about her granddaughter's medical career. Last-moment words are a challenge to comprehend. The instruction was clear: "Careen, do your job." It was a call of desperation, a call for help, as she looked at Dr Careen. Even as Neddie died, Careen could not come to terms with the words left by her granny. Careen had to be wheel chaired as she became slump. I am sure Careen felt total helplessness and hopelessness amidst the circumstances. As a doctor, she would continue to be propelled by those words in her dealings with all the patients who visit her surgery and other places where she works.

Irene Neddie Muyambi left this world in pain and anguish, surrounded by doctors. In relation to her faith, Neddie believed that angels were there waiting to receive her and take her away from this world of torture, suffering, anguish, pain, hatred, jealousy, and so forth. Furthermore, as per her faith, the angels took her to paradise, where she awaits Judgement Day. From graveside speeches, it became clear to me that Neddie was supposedly an angel who lived on earth, did nothing but good, and demonstrated peace, forgiveness, and love for one's neighbour, especially those who are needy. If Neddie's life was not a living testimony to many of us, all we need to do is to ask her to pray for us. But that can no longer be done, because she is no longer linked to us. She is gone. *Goodbye, Neddie.*

Funeral Procedure

Neddie's body was taken from Avenues Clinic to Nyaradzo funeral parlour. Neddie had a policy with Nyaradzo Funeral Assurance Company. They therefore provided services as per her policy, including transporting her body from the clinic to the funeral parlour. It also included a coffin, a hearse, and a bus, and $200 cash to be given to her surviving spouse, Lazarus. Lazarus and Sister Phoebe (CZM) are both beneficiaries of Neddie's policy. The cost of the coffin was $800, but Neddie's children topped up that amount with $2,000 and bought a coffin worth about $3,000. Her children had looked after her, providing her needs whenever she asked. Therefore, they thought it fitting to give her a good send-off too. Neddie's body was transferred from Nyaradzo funeral parlour in Harare to the Gokwe branch, where the body stayed overnight.

About Neddie

Neddie attended Loving and Caring Members (LCM) meetings. She attended Mothers' Union (MU) meetings. Each organisation had different meetings, and she facilitated most of these. At MU conferences and Lady Day gatherings, Neddie's voice was angelic as she led the singing and brought life to everyone present. Neddie was a people person. She rejoiced with those who were rejoicing, for instance at weddings, graduations, and birthday parties.

Neddie mourned with those who were mourning, spending sleepless nights on the floor, giving the people comfort, sometimes in unfavourable conditions. Neddie braved it all. She was the best mum to her family and in-laws, the latter of whom viewed her not as a daughter in-law but as a mum. She had a passion for her job. Though she was a retired teacher, she headed a preschool.

Neddie's desire was to see all the independent projects taken on by her and her husband completed. The clinic was the last one she'd seen the completion of before her death. Her last worry, up until the time of her death, was that if she could handle the title deeds for the projects she had tirelessly and selflessly worked to build over the years. She should be looking down now and saying, "I did a good job. I fought a good fight. I await my crown."

From the speeches, I learnt that Neddie was a comforter to those who were troubled. She was a mediator to those who were in dispute and conflict. She spoke the gospel of forgiveness, and she evidently forgave those who sinned against her. She showed love to her enemies, giving them food when they were hungry and water when they were thirsty. She extended the hand of peace to her adversaries.

She extended the hand of peace to those who sought war with her, especially those who fought to dispossess her of her hard-won achievements, such as the shelter she had built for the needy. What a peaceful woman she was. To those who took advantage of her good heart and humility, this is the time to ask for forgiveness from God, because you might never see Neddie again.

Neddie was a household name. Even her husband called her Neddie until death did them part. She encountered grievous temptations when she engaged in the noble gesture of starting the Community of the Gifts of the Holy Fire with her husband. But the virtuous woman will be remembered for her graciousness and love for God, a love that surpassed all human understanding and that kept her heart within the scope of God's grace. It is Neddie's forgiveness that saw her through all her challenges. She will be remembered for her forgiving nature and her peacefulness. Her works will testify after her. Her strong faith in God and the Trinity, her endurance in hard times, and her encouraging nature will forever be remembered. She worked as a team with other residents and colleagues in the fields. They worked hard to grow all sorts of crops, vegetables and fruits alike, both for food and income. Her fruits of the Spirit—patience, love, forgiveness, gentleness, honesty, and humility—will live after Neddie in those who learnt something from her.

Great appreciation goes to the Community of the Gifts of the Holy Fire Trust, Blue Coat School in Harborne, St Peter's Parish in Harborne, Edgbaston Girls' High School, Birmingham City Council, St Paul's Anglican Church, Bordesley Green, St Stephen's Anglican Parish in Rednal, St George's Parish in Newtown, the church at Junction 10 Walsall, all of whom tirelessly supported Neddie and Lazarus in their work by sending vans, computers, clinic equipment, furniture, and all the other things needed to make the Gokwe projects a success. These projects were all made possible by Neddie's children providing funds to help their parents build and sustain this wonderful place in Gokwe. Neddie's daughter Tsitsi Dorcas Jongwe wrote a book, *Christian Healing Mission in Gokwe, Zimbabwe: A Success Story*, that has been sold to also raise money to develop the projects.

It was clear from the farewell speeches delivered at Neddie's funeral that all who visited the Healing Centre received comfort and encouragement from Neddie. People in wheelchairs came to say goodbye. People walking on crutches, others crawling on their knees, came to say goodbye. One of these people was John Marumisa, who had been healed of leprosy. One could see agony written on everyone's faces, including those who were fighting to dispossess Neddie of her projects.

Neddie will be missed and remembered by all, and her good works will be cherished by many forever and ever. She lives on through her children. She lives on through those who admired her. Her submissiveness as a wife and a helper of the man of God will be missed, as it was admired by all who encountered her. Most people fail to do God's work because they have jealous spouses, but Neddie promoted God's work, not her feelings. She was a respectful wife who, even in her last moments, asked Sister Phoebe and the CZM to take care of Lazarus as founder of the CZM. On the Sunday she became critically ill, she cooked porridge for her husband. Wherever Neddie visited, her excuse for leaving early was her husband's health. She cared for Lazarus, nourished him, and loved him. Neddie was a model to everyone, and her marriage was a model to many married people. She was an inspiration even to her married children, who have kept their vows. Neddie had a character to emulate and resemble. Her legacy will live forever and ever. Amen.

From the speeches, it was clear that Neddie never missed the birthdays of her children, her sons- and daughters-in-law, or her grandchildren. She would phone them anywhere in the world and sing to them.

Neddie singing with her children

The family are going to miss this at future birthdays. They are going to miss the melodious voice of love and care. Neddie's family supported her financially and materially, providing for her personal needs and also materials required for building the Healing Centre. She was well looked after. She wore international clothing—African, United Kingdom, United States, and Australian style. Neddie was a proud mother of children who, as is written in the Bible, will live longer on earth for respecting their parents.

Neddie's Children Arrive in Zimbabwe

Neddie's children arrived from Australia and the United Kingdom at the Harare International Airport in Zimbabwe on 22 and 23 November. They were welcomed by family and Loving and Caring Members (LCM), the latter of whom are third-order members in support of CZM. They were taken to Mr and Mrs Nhamoinesu's homestead in Mainway Meadows, Harare, where they met with relatives from Wedza. These relatives, along with other people, travelled to Gokwe the next day, together with Neddie's three sons and one daughter. Two daughters remained in Harare to process their mother's paperwork before leaving for Gokwe.

After all the paperwork had been done and relatives and friends had gathered at the Nyaradzo funeral parlour to board the Nyaradzo bus, which was filled to capacity, Neddie's body set off for Gokwe. Chiwoniso Dorothea and Tsitsi Dorcas accompanied their mother's body to Gokwe South in the Midlands region.

Preparation and Plans for Burial in Gokwe

Neddie's relatives identifying her body

A meeting was held, attended by Reverend Canon Lazarus Muyambi, Izwi, Muyamuri, and the acting priest in charge, Father Mazula, who was later joined by Reverend John Makiwa, chaplain for the girls' high school. During this planning meeting, the bishop of the Diocese of Central Zimbabwe, Ishmael Mukuwanda, phoned the acting priest in charge and asked if he would pass on his condolences to Lazarus. The bishop was apprised of the burial plans. He informed Reverend Lazarus that he would be returning home ahead of the schedule of the Episcopal Synod to attend Neddie's funeral. The bishop was given an offer to preach at this funeral, which he accepted. He was also informed of the celebrants and those who were going to undertake the committal.

On Thursday, 24 November, Izwi and family took the acting priest in charge, Father Mazula, along with Reverend Makiwa, Reverend Siyachiutuka, and Reverend Makamure, to show them Neddie's final resting place.

Neddie's relatives mark her gravesite

Neddie's Body Arrives in Gokwe

There to welcome Neddie's body were Reverend Canon Lazarus Muyambi (Neddie's husband), her three children Izwi, Idi, and Muyamuri Michael, her adopted child Lawrence, other relatives, some church members, close friends, and people from all the other independent departments at the Healing Centre.

Neddie's body arrived at Gokwe Centre at 6 p.m. There was a viewing, during which time family and close friends identified the body. Her body lay at the Nyaradzo funeral parlour in preparation for burial. The following day, Friday, 25 November 2016, the body was prepared and dressed for burial. There was a church service to hand over the body to the family. Neddie's body was dressed in her Mothers' Union uniform. She had her cross of Jesus on. Her CZM uniform was nicely folded and put to the side. On top of the coffin was another cross. Many people came to the parlour. It was a long convoy to St Agnes Anglican Parish and the Tashaya residence homestead.

Neddie lay in state in her house for three hours before being transferred to the Zimbabwe Healing Centre, Trinity Chapel, where she lay in state for the rest of the night. It was speaker after speaker, song after song, until 6 a.m. on Saturday, 26 November 2016, as the gathering continued to swell, with people vying to sing the praises of a woman who had looked after nuns since the inception of the CZM, the praises of a woman who had served God and the community, a woman who had looked after orphans and fed them in an economically strained Zimbabwe, a woman who had looked after the crippled, the blind, the deaf, and the dumb, a woman who had given shelter to epileptics and lepers who had been abandoned by their families. Neddie was a selfless woman who shared her income with the needy people as she supported in the building of the Healing Centre. Even the parish church that today's congregation enjoys using, Neddie had a hand in building.

The Burial of Neddie

Mourners during the funeral service

On the morning of Saturday, 26 November 2016, all roads in Gokwe led to the Zimbabwe Healing Centre, where Neddie was to be buried. First to arrive was the bishop of the Diocese of Central Zimbabwe and his wife, Elizabeth. They paid their respects at the Tashaya residence before proceeding to the Burial Department of the Healing Centre. Over 1,500 people, arriving in more than 120 cars, and over 65 clergymen from Anglican and other denominations, came to lay Neddie to rest.

Those who came to pay their final respects were from different denominations. Reverend Gwese from the Diocese of Harare was the celebrant and Father Mazula was the co-celebrant during the Requiem Mass. Bishop Ishmael Mukuwanda was the preacher.

After the viewing, Neddie's body was carried by the clergy wives, and later by the family, to the Zimbabwe Trinity Chapel, where she lay in state overnight. This was to be her final resting place. After prayers, Neddie's body was lowered into a nicely dug grave by the altar. The grave had iron rods across it and zinc sheets as a roof. It was filled in with a concrete mixture and floored the next day. Flowers and portraits were put around the grave.

What a well-deserved send-off to one of the most wonderful women of this generation. It was very consoling to all whose lives Neddie had touched. She deserved it.

Vision of an Angel and Reverend Lazarus by the Tashaya Residence

A month before Neddie's death, the students who boarded at Logos High School, living in a dormitory near the Tashaya residence, saw an angel suspended in the air by the Tashaya residence gate. It shone so bright that the girls jumped, collapsing the fence, to get a good glimpse of this heavenly image that appeared to be praying for Lazarus, who was kneeling but suspended in the air as well. This amazed everyone who saw it.

Logos High School girls bid farewell to Neddie

It is widely believed that this appearance of an angel meant that a big mishap was going to take place and that Lazarus was going to be strengthened after his wife's departure.

The Bishop of the Diocese of Central Zimbabwe, Ishmael Mukuwanda, Delivers the Sermon at the Funeral Service

Bishop Mukwanda emphasised how tragic and difficult the loss of Neddie was. He stated that he'd thought she would have a long life, saying that only God knew the number of days she would have. Furthermore, the bishop gave gratitude to Neddie's husband, Lazarus Muyambi, particularly for holding the funeral/burial on Saturday so that he could attend. He said the important thing is not to lead prayers, adding that in a time like this one, God is in charge. He said that just being there to mourn with the other mourners was very important to him. He said that the family of the Province of Central Africa had sent their condolences to the bereaved family. Fifteen bishops and other members of the clergy had also received the tragic news and sent their deepest commiserations. The bishop quoted Isaiah 55:8–9: "'For my thoughts are not your thoughts, neither are your ways my ways,' declares the Lord. 'As the heavens are higher than the earth, so are my ways higher than your ways and my thoughts than your thoughts.'"

**Bishop of Central Zimbabwe preaching
at Neddie's funeral service**

In his sermon, the bishop emphasised that it's hard to understand God's plan. He said that he'd always asked Neddie about Reverend Lazarus's health, and indicated that, sadly, God had taken the nurse and left the patient. He went on to say that on his last visit to St Agnes Parish on 23 October 2016, when he came for confirmation, he had not seen Neddie. He inquired about her whereabouts and was informed that she had gone to Wedza for a funeral. Neddie was a person who committed her life to running around attending to different responsibilities, visiting the sick, and comforting those who were mourning

The bishop said that those present had lost one of their loved ones, as Neddie had been taken away. He said that we may keep asking God why it happened this way but that we need to glorify God in every situation.

The bishop went on to say that, the fact that Neddie was in church on 20 November 2016, the Sunday when she fell seriously ill, emphasised the strength of her faith, because some of us do not attend church when we are unwell or when we have visitors. The bishop said that he asked God what he would be doing on the day of his own death. Neddie was taken while doing God's deeds; what about us? The bishop's wish was for all of us to remember Neddie, who had travelled her journey very well. He stated that on all the occasions when he met the Muyambi couple in the years prior, he observed Lazarus' work, and admired Lazarus for casting out demons who inhabited people.

There is nothing as difficult as being a priest's wife, because priests can be a challenge. Priests' wives should have a spirit of discernment so they can see whether the spirit in their husband is a spirit of truth or not. Neddie was not absent from MU gatherings. She raised people's spirits and motivated most mothers to worship God in spirit and in truth.

Canon Muyambi, who endowed a stipend as a priest and Neddie, who was a teacher, provided for the CZM girls. For most men when they receive phone calls, their wives want to know where the call is coming from, especially if it's from another woman, but Neddie kept these girls in her house. This made her quite unique, because most women wouldn't be able to handle such a situation. She was a truly amazing person. She was a strong woman who persevered through every difficulty. She managed to handle all the responsibilities that came with her role as the wife of a parish priest. The bishop stated that this must not have been easy for her. Therefore, he concluded, she was the caring comforter.

> But what does it matter? The important thing is that in every way, whether from false motives or true, Christ is preached. And because of this I rejoice.
>
> Yes, and I will continue to rejoice, for I know that through your prayers and God's provision of the Spirit of Jesus Christ what has happened to me will turn out for my deliverance. I eagerly expect and hope that I will in no way be ashamed, but will have sufficient courage so that now as always Christ will be exalted in my body, whether by life or by death. For to me, to live is Christ and to die is gain. If I am to go on living in the body, this will mean fruitful labor for me. Yet what shall I choose? I do not know! I am torn between the two: I desire to depart and be with Christ, which is better by far; but it is more necessary for you that I remain in the body. Convinced of this, I know that I will remain, and I will continue with all of you for your progress and joy in the faith, so that through my being with you again your boasting in Christ Jesus will abound on account of me.

Life Worthy of the Gospel

Whatever happens, conduct yourselves in a manner worthy
of the gospel of Christ. Then, whether I come and see you
or only hear about you in my absence, I will know that you
stand firm in the one Spirit, striving together as one for the
faith of the gospel without being frightened in any way by
those who oppose you. This is a sign to them that they will
be destroyed, but that you will be saved—and that by God.
For it has been granted to you on behalf of Christ not only
to believe in him, but also to suffer for him, since you are
going through the same struggle you saw I had, and now
hear that I still have.

(Philippians 1:18–30)

The bishop explained this reading, relating it to Neddie's
departure. "Her departure will bring glory to this earth. Neddie now
stands in heaven for her own deeds. You will stand for your own deeds.
Most of us forget what is our purpose on earth, for our rewards come
later. Let us always be prepared, for we don't know the day or time."
Furthermore, he stated that, "people can have titles; Neddie was a
comforter, a teacher at a school, a teacher of the community, and a
nurse and dietician to her husband. To the Muyambi family, CZM,
and the diocese, it's not going to be business as usual. We don't know
what the family will do. The children are going to arrange the way
forward, since their mother, 'the reporter' who kept them updated in
regard to the Gokwe Mission and their father's health, is no longer
with us. Her position in this place will be hard to fill.

Mothers' Union (MU) members can speak of Neddie's deeds.
She was the coordinator and executive member of the organisation.
She raised the image of God. Knowing how hard some MU members
could be, she used her own money to pay for different assets. For
instance, she bought a steel pot and presented it as Gokwe MU's
contribution. She selflessly did good for others, for the glory of her
branch.

Neddie accompanied Lazarus all over Gokwe doing God's work,
and they worked by themselves to bring the light to Gokwe. Neddie
was a rightful helper to Lazarus. After coming home from their

ventures, she tended to her family. It would have been good for Neddie to stay on earth, but her crown awaited her. Most of us are afraid of death because we don't know where we are going to (Psalm 35:5)."

In addition the Bishop said, "May God's spirit comfort Lazarus and the family. The one who brought Neddie amongst you has taken her. Neddie served everyone when she was in agony, but she did not show her pain; she strived and carried on. Even on that Sunday, she went to church when she was unwell, suppressing her suffering. She suffered critically for twenty-four hours, and then she was gone." The bishop further said, "It's up to God now to give Neddie eternal rest, as she is resting after her good works. In the name of the Father, the Son, and the Holy Spirit. Amen."

Izwi's Speech Delivered at the Funeral

I stand before you humbly representing the Muyambi children. I know today we are bidding farewell to a lady most of you know as that pillar of strength to the children, that pillar of strength to the Mothers' Union, that pillar of strength to the community of St Agnes Mission and the people of Gokwe.

My mum was born on 14 April 1941, having turned seventy-five in April of 2016. She was born into a family of four, and she was the only one remaining after the other three siblings had passed on. Her parents had died as well. My mum and my dad married in 1960 and had six biological children and one adopted child. My mum was a trained primary schoolteacher, and she taught in various schools. After retiring, she worked as head teacher at the preschool.

One of her greatest motherhood attributes was that she never failed to call us on our birthdays, sometimes as early as 5 a.m., and sing "Happy Birthday." That is going to be missed. She phoned us in the United Kingdom, not caring about the expense, but wanting to hear her children's and grandchildren's voices. During our time in Zimbabwe, she visited us without fail. Mum taught us to pray every morning and evening, and she taught us to sing prayerfully and in spirit. She said it was a good way of inviting the Holy Spirit.

Today's gathering is a true reflection and testimony of how far and wide   Mum's love extended and transcended globally.   O u r pillar is now gone after a short illness that lasted twenty-four hours. That soft, whispering voice is no longer with us. Yes, to many of you she held a special place in your hearts, but to us, her children, she was everything and more. When all is said and done, she was all we needed. She was a mother, a friend, an encourager, and a comforter. She was a very solid, sacrificial, no-nonsense person who mentored us to be what you see in us today. She was our schoolteacher at one point or another because she taught at Gokwe School, which we all attended.

My mum and dad founded all these projects you see today. You may want to be reminded of all the projects she devoted herself to.

St Agnes Parish

My mum came to this place in 1972 with our father. At that time there was only one structure, an incomplete priest's house, and the rest was a field. Over the years, in response to God's further instruction, my parents built this place into what it is today. As children we might spend days with very little to eat or to wear, because almost all Mum's savings went towards building these structures you see surrounding you and towards feeding people from all walks of life.

The Church

We used to fetch water a mile away at Ruhwaya, to be used for building the parish church, until the church was completed.

The Convent

Our house, the rectory, was the first convent, as we lived there and shared everything with the nuns.

The complete building of the convent was done with Mum's help and supervision. She supervised the moulding of the bricks and the building of the whole complex. She became the comforter of the nuns as they went through times of trial during their vocation.

The Monastery

Mum also supervised the planning and building of the monastery.

The Orphanage

Our house, the rectory, was the first orphanage, where all coming orphans were housed, clothed, and fed. Neddie was their mother and our mother too. I cannot recall what went on in our minds at that time. I also wonder what went on in Mum's mind at that time. She was a pivotal pillar and foundation to the birth of the orphanage. Mum was the foundation of all plans, including the building and completion of the buildings, which in recent years included the CZM Primary School, the Zimbabwe Healing Centre, the Logos High School, the preschool, and the Healing and Medical Clinic. Mum was a professional full-time teacher, but she managed to get these projects running, as well as to fulfil her role for the government as a teacher. Mum clocked many miles in her entire life. I cannot tell you how many miles, but you can guess. If she managed to come to your house, wedding, funeral, party, or church, you knew she was on the move.

Gokwe Community

Mum was involved in local groups, associations, and councils doing volunteer work. She was involved in non-profit activities and did charitable work for the Gokwe community from the time it was Matabeleland Diocese to the present day, when it is Central Zimbabwe Diocese. She did all this for a cause and to fulfil her calling. Mum has worked with five bishops and three archbishops in the province.

Her work brought value to the community and not distress; she cared about the concerns of local communities and knew how important it was for people to feel they were being loved and cared for. Mum believed in communication as the spice of a good life; she believed in listening to people and trying to act on their concerns. She had an open-door policy, allowing anyone from any walk of life to visit with her and have a drink and something to eat, such as fruits. As you arrived at the residency garden chairs, you were assured of a smile, some food to eat, and a listening ear. Mum and Dad formed a strong bond that the locals thrived on. It was cherished by all people.

Sadly today, when everything has fallen into place, Mum has been denied that joy that every mother gets at childbirth. We accept as children that God's ways are not our ways. Maybe this is how God meant it to be. We believe that our mother, all the same, fought a good fight and ran a good race. Now what awaits her is to receive that precious crown of glory.

We are in tears today. We can feel your tears too. So many questions linger, but it's time to let go. Mrs Muyambi is gone. Mrs Muyambi is no more. She is survived by six children, one adopted child, eighteen grandchildren, and four great-grandchildren.

God has harvested the best flower in the garden. *May her soul rest in eternal peace.*

John's Experience with Neddie

The late Mrs Muyambi was noted for her support of Canon Lazarus Muyambi and all projects, especially the children's home and the Healing Centre. At the Healing Centre, she would redirect people possessed with demons as some ran away or rolled on the floor; and bring them to the Channel of God. During healing sessions, she would lead the singing on her own. To her, singing was paramount, and a crucial factor, because the Holy Spirit was felt during these sessions. I worked with Neddie very well and will miss her.

Neddie was an active participant in whatever she was involved, for example at Gokwe School, were she taught for years as a teacher of music, a subject she had not majored in when she trained as a teacher.

One other thing she will be remembered for is that at church gatherings when people appeared to be low-spirited, she would rise to sing and speak, such that the atmosphere would change to a lively one.

Neddie was no gossiper. Instead she was unifier who wished that differing parties would work together in peace. While she was not in the habit of speaking ill about other people, she rebuked everyone she saw doing bad behaviour, usually on a one-on-one basis. She did not believe in giving anyone a dressing-down in public.

Neddie was consistent in her commitment. For example, up to the last Sunday of her life, she attended church when she was in pain and had difficulty breathing.

Neddie was full of hospitality up to the last day of her life, and she cared for many, including orphans, visitors, and needy people. She was very sympathetic of the bereaved, and she went wherever there was bereavement within the church, amongst family and people she knew or did not know. A week before her death, she spent a night at Edwin Munyoro's funeral about fifteen kilometres away from her home.

· · · · · · · · ●· · · · · · · · · ·

Comment

John lived with Neddie's family from 1974 on. He came as a patient but stayed at the parish learning more about God's work. He was involved in driving out evil spirits, as he worked side by side with Lazarus and Neddie. Up to today, John works at the Healing Centre. He finally became a priest. He also works at Logos High School as a chaplain.

Reverend Makamure Remembers Neddie

I met Mrs Muyambi just a month after my ordination when I was posted to St Agnes in Gokwe. The first time I visited their homestead, I found the family with Reverend L. T. Muyambi sitting in their lounge. We had a talk. As I was about to leave, they said that they would come to my house to officially welcome me as a visitor. After a week, Mrs Muyambi did come. With the aid of one of their workers, the family brought me some food items, including Cokes, bananas, spinach, and sorghum. All I can say is that Mrs Muyambi was a mother to everyone. Even in the few months I spent with her, I saw that she was a mum to the whole congregation. She was a talented singer. This is all I can say about her, as I knew her for only the few months that I had contact with her before she was taken by the Lord.

—Reverend Makamure

Irene Neddie's grave

Reverend Mazula's Wife, Caroline Mazula, Mourns the Death of Neddie

I came to St Agnes Parish in 2007 with my husband, who is the priest in charge here. When I got here, there was an active Mothers' Union (MU) group. By then life was difficult for me, because we had transferred from Zvishavane. I did not have an MU pin. Seeing this, Irene Neddie Muyambi, the wife of the retired priest, gave me a pin. I was so delighted, because an MU pin is part of the uniform and very important. I really felt happy and a full member of the organisation.

We had nice times when we attended MU retreats at St Patrick's Mission in Gweru. I am sure that Neddie liked me and was very happy with me, because throughout the retreats I made sure I provided her with warm water for bathing. Neddie supplied me with goodies. She made me her daughter to the extent that I only had to ask for something I did not have and she would give it to me without question. Each time Neddie expressed great joy in helping me.

The last time we attended the MU conference at St Patrick's, in August, Neddie was very energetic. Little did I know that it the last time we would attend that conference together. She was talented at motivating large gatherings and good at promoting church functions. She motivated everyone to sing. Her voice was angelic.

On Sunday, 20 November, I sat side by side with her in church. She had come late that day, which was unlike her. I did not know that was our last Eucharist together. It really pains me, because part of me is now gone. My husband, who is the priest in charge, did not know that he was celebrating Neddie's last Holy Communion. Neddie had fallen asleep seated on the bench, which is something I had never seen in all the times we had sat together, which we did every Sunday. I had to wake her up to go and receive Holy Communion. She smiled at me with that golden smile she gave to everyone. Neddie walked to the altar, received her last Holy Communion, came back, and sat down for a while, which was also unusual, because normally she rushed home to attend to her poorly husband.

That same Sunday around 6 p.m., My husband and I were informed that Neddie was not feeling well. We rushed to Neddie's home (the Tashaya residence) after 6 p.m., only to be informed that she had been rushed to Gokwe Hospital. We immediately followed the family to the hospital. Upon our arrival at Gokwe Hospital, they were still at the outpatient department. We and the nuns helped the nurses to help get Neddie to the ward. She appeared very weak but was responding to questions. She was having difficulty breathing. I assisted her to take her medication and to make sure she was warm in bed.

I will greatly miss her. Despite our age difference, Neddie was quite accommodating and loving. She was a wonderful woman.

She had time for everyone. Her humility was comparable to none. She was a good advisor. For instance, she would point out when something was not right and needed correction. I say rest in peace, my best friend.

Rhodah Cynthia Madovi Writes about Her Last Encounter with Neddie

On Sunday, 20 November 2016, after Mass and during church notices, Neddie stood up to go home as always. I had not seen her the previous week, so I decided to follow her. I called her to wait for me, so she sat on a bench under a mango tree by the children's home. I ran to her and was really shocked at her laboured breathing. I stood face-to-face with her. We discussed my house in Bulawayo. She advised me that after the schools closed in December, I should go to Bulawayo and get all my paperwork and then return to Gokwe so that I could be fully employed at the Logos clinic since I had experience with clinical work.

I informed Neddie that the parents at Logos Girls' High were eager for sixth form to commence as soon as possible. The parents wanted their children to continue at the same school. I therefore asked Neddie to talk to her husband, Lazarus, about it. One of the orphans, Chipo, arrived as I chatted with Neddie. She mentioned to Neddie that she appeared unwell, but Neddie said she was all right and did not seem to want to discuss her health. Neddie informed me that some years ago, there was a prophetic utterance which said that she and Lazarus should pray for St Agnes Parish. She said their failure to do so was going to result in the closure of the church. Neddie informed me that she and Lazarus, with the help of a few people, had built the church and the other shelters around it. Neddie pointed at all the buildings in the parish and said that she and Lazarus had built them. Her concern was that the new priests and church members who were coming and going should consult her about the history of the parish and about how things are done. If they would ask how Lazarus and Neddie had started their work at the parish, it could help them run the church.

The church used to be full, but now only nine members are registered and attending. The church is almost empty. I advised Mum to call the current priest and his wife and advise them on how to develop the parish and bring people to church. Neddie said she had the history and was willing to discuss the matter with the incoming priests.

We looked at the rectory, which had big stones on top to stop the roof from being taken by wind. The rectory looked more like ruins. A building is a gift that we should cherish.

I said bye to Mum. She looked at me for a moment without saying anything. I did not realise it was our last moment together. She walked away with Chipo. Chipo supported her to keep her from losing her balance.

—Sencia Rhodah Madovi

Mrs Kambanga Mourns Neddie

Spiritual Work

At church, Neddie was good at preaching. Her sermons were mainly about perseverance, spiritual growth, peace, love, respect and harmony.

She was very much concerned with mothers. Clergy wives got a lot of instruction from her, especially those with husbands at college.

She also usually talked about how to pray. She was worried about how mothers presented themselves before God, especially with regard to their appearance, for instance how they dressed.

As a musician, she could sing hymns and creeds in a harmonious way at church and church gatherings.

She was once appointed by the Mothers' Union (MU) president to be a coordinator for MU in Gokwe South and North. She did very well in leading the MU in both districts.

She was also a comforter of people of all ages, especially widows, nuns, and friars.

She was a good supporter of the church, together with her husband, Canon L. T. Muyambi. They donated things like buildings, computers, clothes, food, utensils, beasts, and other church accessories. Neddie participated fully in all activities and events of the church, for example harvest day, endowment, assessment, tithing, and MU contributions.

Neddie was a deacon and, no matter her age, could assist the priest if there were no servers or even deacons to do so.

She encouraged the members of Mothers' Union to exchange gifts and visit each other to promote good relations within the church.

She encouraged women to donate items for functions like weddings, funerals, and church gatherings.

She encouraged girls to be nuns and boys to be friars.

She encouraged weddings for both single people and couples already living together without being married.

We salute her. Rest in peace, Mother.

Neddie as a Teacher

Neddie was a teacher by profession, specialising in infant education.

She was talented in music such that she conducted the school choir at Gokwe Primary School and reached district level. It was an achievement at that time, since she was the first woman to perform to that level.

Her classroom was a talking classroom. It was fully furnished with children's learning materials.

Neddie was a good advisor. The school had an advisory board, of which she was a member. She could challenge individual teachers with regard to the way they dressed or behaved at work.

She was always energetic with whatever she did. She had a sense of beauty. Her classroom had flowers throughout the year, even in winter. She would be the only one in the whole school with flowers.

Teachers and children alike enjoyed her school assembly lessons, which were meaningful and spiritual. She could lead demonstration lessons in areas of need. Mathematics was her subject of perfection.

Neddie raised her level of education from Standard Six to ordinary level and encouraged others to further their studies.

Reverend Canon Lazarus Muyambi's Narrative

Neddie and I went to school together at St John's Matsvayi Primary School. This was in the 1940s. Neddie was in Sub A while I was doing Standard Two. We were just school children with no motive at all. Our homes, Mudungwe and Nyaungwa, were about fourteen kilometres apart. We walked long distances to get to school each day.

I left St John's for St Anne's Mission in the early 1950s. Neddie later came to do Standard One while I was doing Standard Three.

Still there was no relationship, but we knew each other as coming from neighbouring villages.

From St Anne's I went to St Paul's Musami, a Catholic school, to do Standard Five and Standard Six. At one time the school wanted to convert me and baptise me into the Roman Catholic Church. I refused. This caused a lot of controversy at the mission school. I was dismissed from the school, along with sixteen other students. The principal of the school was then dismissed, having been accused of dismissing us on religious grounds. I then went to St Mary's Hunyani, where I was given a place to do Standard Six the following year. I therefore decided to look for a job in Bulawayo. I found a job as a houseboy.

I then worked for a chemist, and then for a South African timber company in Sixth Avenue, Bulawayo. In December, I went home for Christmas, and in January I went back to St Mary's Hunyani to start my education. The principal, John Ebbs, gave me a warm welcome. I was elected the vice-captain of the school. After I finished my schooling, the principal secured me a place at St Patrick's Secondary School to train as a teacher.

In those two years, I was head server in church. I did very well in my studies. Towards end of second year, I was appointed headmaster to Hwange United School, No. 3 Colliery. I was to work under Reverend Endy Wistle, who was the superintendent at the school. During my time at Hwange, I went to Bulawayo to write an examination for a Junior Certificate at Mzilikazi Government School. I visited Irene Neddie's uncle Bezel Nyahwata, who was my friend from Wedza. He now worked in Bulawayo. At this time, Irene Neddie Mashinya was doing Standard Six at St Patrick's Roman Catholic School in Bulawayo and living with her parents in Barbourfields.

Before proposing love for her, I checked her books. She was doing well academically. I knew that marrying an intelligent wife would lead to intelligent children. I then took my first step towards courting Neddie, and soon we fell in love. I phoned Reverend Adams of St Patrick's Mission in Chiwundura, Gweru, to secure Neddie a place to train as a teacher. I later paid *lobola* (dowry) to Neddie's father in Barbourfields, Bulawayo, Zimbabwe.

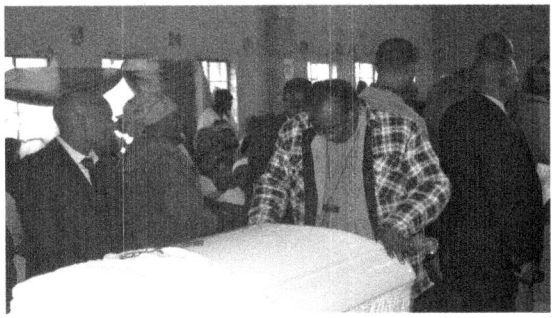

Graduation and Wedding

WEDDING BELLS 17 DEC. 1960

After Neddie's graduation on 5 December 1960, we married the next day at St Columba's Anglican Church Makokoba, in Bulawayo. We had a glamorous wedding on this day, 6 December 1960. It was a really jigsaw puzzle, but eventually everything fell into place. Neddie was a virgin, and the customary procedures were observed. There was an egg atop cornmeal in a small basket (*tswanda*) placed on the altar on the wedding day. The second wedding reception was in Wedza.

In January of 1961, my wife and I left Wedza for Hwange. We were both teaching at Hwange United School, No. 3 Colliery, the new school that I was heading. After a year, someone with better qualifications came to succeed me. In October of the same year, 1961, Neddie and I were blessed with a baby girl, Chiwoniso Dorothea (her name meaning "a gift from God"). She was born at Mpilo Hospital in Bulawayo. In 1963, our second child, Tsitsi Dorcas, was born in Wankie.

Fasting for a Baby Boy

Realising we had two girls, Neddie and I went into the bush to fast and pray, requesting for a baby boy from God our Creator. He came in 1966. We named him Anesu ("God is with us"). While I was at St John's Seminary in Lusaka, Zambia, training as a priest, I heard a voice saying, "*Tichakupazve mumwe mwanamukomana*" (We will give you another boy child). I woke up to check where the voice was coming from, but I saw no one. I sat up in a chair and wrote the message on a piece of paper.

I sent a copy of the letter to my wife, Neddie, who was teaching at St John's Matsvayi in Wedza during the time I was training to be a priest.

In 1969, Neddie and I were blessed with another baby boy. We named him Izwi ("logos"). He was born in Hwange, where we now lived as a family after my ordination as a priest.

Life in Botswana

From 1970 to 1971 we lived in Botswana. I was a full-time priest at St Augustine Parish Church in Serowe. I was also priest in charge of some outstations which I regularly visited for church services. Neddie continued teaching at a nearby school. I used to preach in the London Missionary in Botswana. I was a football referee.

Transfer to Gokwe, Rhodesia

In April of 1972, I and my family transferred to St Agnes Mission in Gokwe, Rhodesia. We entered the rectory through the window. I had to lift and push my children through the window because there was no one to welcome us upon our arrival. This was my second visit, though. For the first visit I had gone by myself, leaving my family in Bulawayo, and had found that the rectory and the church were incomplete. This time around, only the church was incomplete. There was just a laid foundation which had been there for five years. The area of the church was seventy square metres

There was no water for anything, not even to drink. We had to walk a mile to get water from a nearby borehole. My family was not used to this life. They had to carry heavy containers and push drums with capacity of two hundred litres of water for household use. We eventually sank our own well a few metres from the rectory, and we installed a pump. This was done with the help of Bishop Mark Wood. The well still stands today and supplies clean, fresh water to the parish.

The area was full of wild animals. Still today I wonder how no one was attacked. The warthog was a common animal, as were the monkeys that regularly came to steal our harvest. Also, some eerie insects and very dangerous snakes infested the area.

In the same year we moved to Gokwe, my wife started teaching at St Agnes School, now called Gokwe School. She was a very good music trainer and choir mistress. Her choir won in yearly musical competitons. I used to be invited to judge music performance at district- and provincial-level competitions.

Neddie; her mother, Sofia Mashinya; and their granddaughter

My wife, Neddie, started a very active Mothers' Union (MU) group as an enrolling member. She helped me start and establish mission stations around Gokwe district. In the process, she was establishing new MU branches and enrolling new members. Neddie led in all the singing; she was a star and the public liked her. This strengthened our church ministry in the Gokwe district. I was also baptising new converts, and twenty mission stations were established. The new converts were baptised by the different bishops who held office during our time there.

At the same time, I started the healing ministry. Bishop Mark Wood sent two people, Reverend Noel Scott and Reverend Titus Zhenje, to test my gift of healing. It was accepted and approved that God was at work in my ministry. My wife, Neddie, was the principal supporter of this ministry. She really believed in me and loved to see the ministry succeed. Neddie stood by me, singing, teaching confession, fasting, and meditation, and offering herself in prayer all day and or all night.

Building the St Agnes Parish church

We mobilised the community to mould bricks and provide building material for building the church. I informed the bishop that the church was complete and we wanted roofing material. Bishop Mark Wood advised that we make use of the environment, meaning that we cut trees and grass for roofing. I prayed about the matter, and then I went to the ZISCO steel company in Kwekwe. I met ZISCO officials and told them my story in the form of a prayer they listened with a sympathetic ear and as we discussed they answered my cry. They informed me that they were going to prepare the roofing material, including zinc sheets, which they eventually did, delivering the material to St Agnes Parish Church. The priests who were my predecessors at this parish had met with difficulty and encountered resistance from the community. They therefore could not develop further. Unfortunately, the one just before me had died (see *Christian Healing Mission in Gokwe, Zimbabwe: A Success Story*), and soon I was called from Botswana to Gokwe.

The St Agnes Parish Church Building

We used to worship under a tree or in a classroom at the nearby Gokwe School. Once the church was finally complete, it was officially opened in 1973 by the Right Reverend Bishop Mark Wood. We later established an orchard around the church. We used water from our well to water the fruit trees and the flourishing vegetable garden. We were later given land by the headman, Ruhwaya, for farming. We grew different crops, including sunflowers for chicken feed. We kept chickens and cattle. We ate from our orchard, garden, and fields, which made life easier and healthier for my family. We also did bee farming in a small way and ate lots of natural honey.

We shared our harvest with sick people who came for healing at the Centre. We also shared with the orphans, nuns, and the needy. Our parishioners were very good at bringing us food from their harvests. We shared with everyone at the parish, for we were a family united in prayer. Some of the needy people who visited us were the Tonga and the vaShangwe. This forced Neddie and me to create jobs for the Gokwe community. Most of the people during those days were not educated, so Neddie and I started an adult literacy group, and a study and examination centre called Central African Correspondence Centre (CACC), for those willing to further their studies. These were extra gifts we gave to the local people apart from our ministry.

Neddie and I built a convent because some of the girls who were living in our house showed they wanted to serve God. We asked them to help us as nuns, and they agreed. Building a convent would mean that the girls would leave our house and reside in the convent.

The Orphanage

One day I came across a social services worker by the name of Mr Muzuva who was heading a sub-office in Kwekwe. He was holding a small baby while sitting in his office. I said to him, "Why are you nursing a baby in here?" He said the baby's mother had died and the father was ill. Muzuva was going to take the baby to the hospital. He asked me if I would take the baby with me and look after her at our parish. I agreed. I took the baby to our parish and looked after her in our house. Neddie took responsibility for looking after the child, providing all her basic needs. She looked after her like our own child. We named her Rumbidzai ("praise ye the Lord").

**Reverend Lazarus and Irene Neddie (Right),
with carers and orphans**

From then onwards more orphans came to us. Neddie accepted them and looked after them in our house. We later decided to move them into the convent to live in a spare bedroom, where they could be looked after by the nuns. Eventually we built an orphanage and called it the St Agnes Children's Home. It was registered with the government of Zimbabwe as C.R. 772 and was officially opened by the Deputy Minister of Labour, Manpower, Planning, and Social Welfare, Comrade Florence Chitauro, on 2 May 1992. Present was the venerable archdeacon Junious Gwekwerere.

The Zimbabwe Healing Centre:
Trinity Zimbabwe Chapel

The healing ministry started in the 1960s. But in the 1970s, when I got to Gokwe, it was renewed. One day I visited Gokwe Hospital and found Mrs Priscinia Munyoro, a mother to one of our Nuns, Sister Eugenia, suffering from painful legs. She was discharged. I drove her to her home fifteen kilometres away and laid hands on her legs. I prayed for her healing. As I prayed, her leg was shaking.

In another healing incident, Mrs Chimhou (Sister Gladys's mother) complained of pain in her legs. I laid hands on her leg, which started shaking. She was healed after a long illness.

Where there is a great man, there is a greater woman behind him. Without the tireless support of my wife, Neddie, this healing ministry wouldn't have taken off the ground. Neddie's part was very important. She would handle those who were falling and running away under possession of evil spirits. Neddie sang powerfully when I prayed for the sick. Her angelic voice will be forever missed.

• • • • • • • • • ● • • • • • • • • • •

The area we lived in was full of trees, so constructing small huts for the sick was not a problem. And firewood was abundant. Sick people were trickling in and being accommodated. They lived at the Healing Centre for seven days or more before being discharged. Those with serious ailments stayed longer. They would attend morning service (matins), midday prayers called Angelus, and evensong and Sunday church services. They engaged in fasting, prayer, meditation, and Bible reading. They suffered from incurable medical illnesses like leprosy, epileptic fits, heavy dizziness, bad dreams, and evil spirit possession. Some were haunted by alien spirits, witches, wizards, or witch doctors. Witches were found in a place called Gandavaroyi in Gokwe. In those days, darkness covered the whole area of Gokwe. The people who dwelled in darkness had seen light. Gokwe definitely needed deliverance. I was invited to schools to perform exorcisms because school children were being possessed by evil spirits and going hysteric.

It was a great learning experience for me and Neddie, getting to know evil spirits better and challenging them. Neddie sometimes would sprinkle holy water on a possessed person in order to calm them down.

The sick people who lived at the Healing Centre engaged in farming and gardening in addition to their life of prayer. This life has continued until today. Those with mental illnesses stayed longer as well. Neddie was a mother to them all. All the sick people knew they had a mother who reassured them, comforted them, and provided for them.

Bishop Murindagomo travelled all the way from Mutare to witness this work. He was satisfied and wrote a letter to the World Council of Churches informing them of the healing ministry and of God being at work in Gokwe. We were doing this healing ministry in the company of angels and the Holy Spirit. My wife, Neddie, was protected, but one day she was attacked on the leg by a devil. The injury appeared like a black spot. Her leg caused her a great deal of pain. I prayed for her and she was healed.

In 1973, our fifth child was born. We named her Idi ("truth of God"). Our last child was born in 1977, in Gokwe. Neddie was pregnant after having received advice from the holy angels. In the ninth month of her pregnancy, we had visitors, Reverend Mbuvayesango and Bishop Murindagomo. Neddie went into labour. A nurse surprisingly arrived from nowhere and assisted Neddie in delivering the baby. We named our son Muyamuri Michael, as we had been instructed by the archangels Michael and Raphael before his birth. It was surprising that the angels gave him a Shona name. It was said that Muyamuri Michael would do greater works than I had done (see *Christian Healing Mission in Gokwe, Zimbabwe: A Success Story*).

Later on, in the 1980s, Neddie and I adopted a boy child and called him Lawrence Lazarus.

Wilson Sitshebo

Wilson worked with me as an adult literacy teacher. He lived in a round hut near the rectory. Later in life he studied for his PhD in theology and became the bishop of Matabeleland. He was a good friend of the family. During his time as bishop of Matabeleland, he invited my daughter Tsitsi Dorcas to address a diocesan Mothers' Union conference on HIV/AIDS. Dorcas at that time was the Central Zimbabwe Diocese coordinator for HIV/AIDS.

Wilson Sitshebo helped in my healing ministry, together with John Makiwa and my wife, Neddie. They worked side by side. It was a big job that required teamwork. At that time, the evil spirits were a challenge, but later in life they quietly departed as I laid hands on people. This was probably because there was more healing power and more angels to control the situation. Today we do no longer experience such challenges.

John Makiwa

Reverend John Makiwa (second from left)

John Makiwa, a former delivered person, now helps me to pray for the sick. He was very close to my wife, Neddie. She and I lived with John for many years. After his deliverance, John went to train as a teacher. He also earned a degree in theology through distance learning. John is a devoted person who has stood firm in his work for God.

He was later ordained as a priest.

Friars and Nuns

Neddie remained mother to all. Every department called Neddie *Mum*. The outside community called her *Mum*. She will be missed by all.

We relocated from the parish house as instructed by the holy angels in 1984. We built our eight-roomed house half a kilometre away from the parish house. God wanted us to live a distance away from the parish house. We were informed by the holy angels that the nuns would work in our house because Neddie and I were very busy people. Also, we were asked to go to my original home in Wedza and sell all our belongings. We therefore sold our house, cattle, shop, grinding mill, and other, small things, and came to live permanently in Gokwe. This was in obedience to God. Our new home, the Tashaya residence, has a big orchard, beautiful flower and vegetable gardens, and a well with good fresh water.

The nuns who came to work at our house were accused of committing many different negative behaviours. We therefore stopped them from coming to our house. This was for the good of God's work. Their behaviour towards me was also suspicious. Some nuns left the community of their own accord, just like the friars who left the community in order to marry. Others left for employment and greener pastures. They left after we had sacrificed all our resources for their own good, hoping the community would benefit from their education. After we gave them an education, we sent some of them to work and study abroad. Teachers, priests, carpenters, welders, nurses—all left for a different life. This was a big blow, because the community never benefitted from them. It only shows that single people can be a real challenge to manage. We, however, continue to accept new postulants at the convent. We believe that our rewards will come from God. I am convinced Neddie is enjoying her rewards after death, because life did not reward her. The nuns are now divided into two groups. Some are at St Patrick's Gweru, and others have remained loyal to the founder in Gokwe. Two nuns are working abroad; they have completely abandoned their Gokwe community. We gave them an education hoping they would support the community, but we continue to struggle financially without their support. We worry about those with double standards, because they are detrimental to our existence.

One of the nuns who left us after a long period of working with us was Sister Gladys Chimhou. She is currently based at St Patrick's Mission as a matron for the secondary school. She and other nuns and friars live and work at the mission school. They have mobilised themselves against the work at Gokwe. Neddie accepted all this and only prayed for them daily. I am sure she is praying for them in heaven. Despite the treatment she received from them, she continued to do good for them. She used to bring them some fruits each time she visited them at St Patrick's for meetings. What a gifted woman of God she was. Over the years, Sister Gladys has left us but has returned after hearing God's voice instructing her to come back to Gokwe. When she left this time, it was not in our jurisdiction to bring her back. We just wait upon the Lord, who has brought her back in the past.

Building Schools

Neddie and I agreed to build a primary school and a secondary school. Neddie taught at CZM Primary School before retiring. She was the pre-school headmistress at the time of her death. Our aim was to empower the girl child whose plight was compromised and who was looked down upon in the Zimbabwean environment. We wished to change the focus of a girl child from marriage as the first goal to academic excellence. We wanted the girl child to feel accepted in this male-dominated society and to feel she can achieve against all odds.

CZM Primary School

A girl should not be a sexual object, as she is a vessel to be valued and respected. She is not cheap labour and is not to be ridiculed and humiliated.

We have the best staff in the schools to empower our students.

Our matrons are disciplinarians, disciplining students in the way that pleases God. We want the girl child to stand up and be heard. I shall try to carry on without Neddie, who was a rightful helper given by God.

Logos Secondary School

Gone but Never Forgotten

Neddie was laid to rest in the Trinity Chapel. It rained the entire day of her funeral. Over seventeen-hundred people gathered, including more than sixty-five priests. More than 165 cars were there. There might have been more people if it had not rained. The reasons for such rains? Only God knows why he opened the skies all morning until Neddie was in her tomb, well laid to rest in a chapel, a practice that is common in some countries. It is an honour given to those who have provided outstanding service to the church. Neddie will forever be missed.

The Health and Healing Medical Clinic

Nurses at the new clinic in Gokwe

Our aim in building a clinic was to make sure the Gokwe community was well catered for in terms of health. The health system in Zimbabwe has collapsed; therefore, we aim at bridging the gap by providing better services to our community. A person's health is more important than money; hence, our projects are non-profit. The human being created by God is our priority. We also aim to create employment opportunities for our community. We have security guards at the Centre to make sure everyone is safeguarded.

Neddie was sweet and righteous. She left me as a widower. I feel hopeless and helpless. I was so devastated that I thought dying myself was a better option than continuing to live. What would life be like without Neddie? She is irreplaceable. Even on the day she became critically ill, she worried more about me than about herself. She left me with six children and one adopted child. Many more orphans she looked after are in the world. I wonder if they care about us anymore.

Reverend Lazarus and Irene Neddie

Neddie was the type of wife described in Proverbs 31. "Who can find a good wife?" She cared for me. She met all my needs. We cared for each other throughout our fifty-seven years of marriage. The years brought bread, butter, fruit, and tomatoes to our table. I loved her so much. She respected me and my position as a priest. In good and challenging times alike, she remained a strong pillar to lean on.

Reverend Lazarus and Irene Neddie

One year we visited Jerusalem and saw wonderful places. We really enjoyed our stay in Israel, seeing where Christ was born, crucified, and buried. We had opportunities to visit the United Kingdom as a couple. On another visit there, we took Muyamuri Michael. He attended preschool at the time. Neddie was doing communication studies. I was doing healing sessions with other channels of healing based in the United Kingdom. We went to Burswood in Kent, a big healing centre in the UK. They still write me today, inviting me over. They wanted me to stay permanently in the UK, but the work of God was waiting for me in Zimbabwe. They gave us £450 to come and buy a car to use in our healing ministry. I used to give lectures and also heal sick people there.

I prayed for a Russian girl and she was healed in Jesus's name. I also prayed for Dorothy Karen. After her death, I visited the UK. The last time I visited UK, family had invited us. We had good times going to the beach and relaxing on the sands.

In 2015 Neddie and I celebrated our fifty-fourth wedding anniversary, solemnised by Bishop Ishmael Mukuwanda. It was a great day for Neddie and me. For our honeymoon, we went on a two-week cruise of Lake Kariba up to Victoria Falls. It was one of the most refreshing trips I have ever had.

My life with Neddie was a life of helping people. She was very kind and helped different people from all walks of life, including the handicapped and the abandoned.

**Reverend and Irene Neddie celebrating
55th Wedding Anniversary**

She was a mother to my siblings, including my two sisters who are profoundly deaf. Neddie was very kind and helpful to my mother and father. She loved them until their departure from this world.

The whole clan from my home area in Wedza came to say goodbye to their beloved daughter-in-law. One speaker after another spoke of Neddie's good works, good heart, and hospitality, and how she was more of a mother to them than an in-law. They spoke of how Neddie visited them in times of crisis, death, or illness. In times of celebration, Neddie was there too. She was a people person, performing acts of mercy to all during times of illness and death. She stood for us all.

Reverend Muyambi's late parents

All our children were married in the church. They were our comforters then, and even today as I speak, they are my comforters. They have stood by me during my grief over losing their beautiful mother. I have received so much comfort.

I used to go with Neddie to Harare for health check-ups and for consultations when she was not feeling well. I used to accompany her to private doctors or hospital. We had check-ups done on us by Doctor Matenga in Harare, a good mature doctor. Neddie's was an untimely death. The suddenness of it did not give me the opportunity to care for her or help her recover. Mrs Partners and Sister Eugenia were present at home with me when my wife became seriously ill. My children in the UK advised me to take Neddie to hospital immediately, which I did.

The ambulance from Harare caused the delay in my wife's getting expert help in Harare. We had an active medical aid programme—CIMAS. My wife was entitled to an air rescue from Gokwe to Harare. My heart is wounded. Neddie left me when I needed her most.

I was not well, but I became stronger for her. It was I who was meant to die, not Neddie. She was stronger, and I was unwell. After her burial in our own Trinity Chapel, which we built, my children took me to Harare, where my granddaughter Dr Careen had secured emergent booking with the specialist Dr Ngwende. She also booked me with CIMAS Surgery. Doctor Muriva referred me to the specialist doctor at whose office I had my head scanned, my pelvis scanned, my chest x-rayed, and my blood tests performed. In fact, I had a complete medical check-up. I was given all the medication required. At age eighty-two, I was pronounced fit and in sound health.

Neddie was a deputy superintendent at the orphanage. Her death has left a void that will be difficult to fill. She deserved the honour of being buried in a chapel because of her good works in the healing ministry, looking after orphans and looking after and providing for the needy people of this age and time. She was a good leader, musician, and church choir conductor, as she was sober-minded and kind-hearted, caring for poor people, especially the Tonga and the vaShangwe people of Gokwe. Sometimes she bought stuff she had no intention of using herself, just to help others. Neddie welcomed strangers into our house. She never sent anyone away empty-handed. She gave clothes to the needy and paid fees for needy children. She sympathised with people in trouble. She taught girls to remain virgins. She warned women against being sexually abuse by men. She gave them tips on how to look after themselves. That's why she started and supported St Agnes Guild.

Neddie never caused trouble or brought trouble to me. She never shouted or scolded or even exchanged bad words with anyone. Neddie was an advisor and a counsellor. At one stage we were invited to go and counsel a couple having a dispute. My wife calmly dealt with the couple. She patched up marriages. She was against marriage-breaking, marriage-wrecking, and marriage-distracting spirits. She warned couples against such demonic spirits. The Holy Spirit does not live where there is chaos, quarrelling, and discord. Couples should strive to uphold peace in their marriages. A family that prays together stays together. She encouraged couples to calmly solve their disputes. Prayer is the answer to any impediment. Many married couples came to Neddie for help. She used to advise me not to fight. One day I fought someone, and she came and removed my glasses. This was in Kwekwe. I was very angry with this person who had fixed my car. He had lied, saying that it was not ready, yet he was driving it up and down Kwekwe, transporting people and charging them. Neddie's quiet nature and quiet spirit remains unexplainable to me. She was an angel amongst us, but now she is gone.

Our house was clean and our outdoor garden beautiful. She used to go to the shops to buy bones and vegetables. She cooked good food for me. She always asked people in Harare, Kwekwe, and Gweru to bring greens for me, her loving husband. She monitored my blood pressure and diabetes. She made sure I ate less starch. She fulfilled all marriage vows. She was my friend, wife, advisor, and counsellor. I provoked her sometimes and she did not like it, but she remained steadfast in her love for me. She continued to do good every time, as the Bible says.

Neddie was the love of my life, and I was hers. Her loss has brought great sadness and a massive void that will never be filled again. She was my wife, the mother of my children, my companion, and above all my best friend. Neddie loved me very much. I could not stop her from dying. God knows why he took my wife before he took me. I should have been the first one to die, before her. I had more enemies and evil angels than she had. I had many threats from the devil. The devil wanted to dispossess me of all my belongings. I feel my wife died because of medical negligence. If I had been given an opportunity to speak to her in her last moments, I don't know what I could have said. Maybe I would have said, "Neddie, please don't leave me alone."

If I had been with her in her last moments, Neddie might have said, "Father, carry on with the healing ministry, continue to take care of the orphans, and continue fighting for the title deeds for our projects which we have selflessly and tirelessly worked for over the years."

My wife was the most forgiving soul that ever lived. Her forgiving heart was comparable to none; she was a true Christian woman. She will forever be missed. She has left all the work in my hands, yet I thought I was going to leave it in all her hands. Neddie was eight years younger than I, so I was confident she would support me in my old age, which she was already doing. Our work was a direct instruction from God. This should encourage other priests to do work in their ministry apart from just saying Mass and burying the dead. There is so much more work to do in God's field than just saying Mass and sitting in offices.

Doctor's Report

What Really Took Neddie's Life, from a Medical Perspective

Irene Neddie had a long history of high blood pressure. Her kidneys eventually stopped functioning properly, and she therefore had kidney failure. This caused her heart to enlarge, a condition called uraemic pericarditis. Her ineffective heart function made her heart swell, and there was accumulation of fluid in her lungs, which caused difficulty in breathing. All these factors compounded, leading to her death.

Strange Incident at Funeral Gathering in Harare: Handbag Disappears

As soon as Neddie's children arrived at the Harare International Airport, as mentioned earlier on, they were welcomed by family and friends. They were taken to the homestead of Mr and Mrs Nhamoinesu, who are Loving and Caring Members (LCM) doing God's work at the Zimbabwe Healing Centre in Gokwe. When Neddie's children got to the Nhamoinesus' house in Mainway Meadows, Harare, their father's family had arrived from Wedza and were waiting to receive them and grieve with them. All went well. Present were their father's sisters, brothers, cousins, nephews, nieces, uncles, and aunts. They were comforted as each one of them spoke words of condolence, saying how good Neddie had been to them.

Around 10 p.m., one of Neddie's daughters, Tsitsi Dorcas (TD), wanted to go to her daughter's house in Avondale to freshen up, after which point she planned to come back to spend time with everyone else, since they were there for Neddie's family. Having later changed her mind, she got out of the car and asked her daughter to pick her up in the morning. TD opened her handbag, took out a wallet, and handed it over to her daughter. Strangely enough, and very unusual for her, she did not give her passport to her daughter for safekeeping, as she has always done over the years when she has visited Zimbabwe. In her handbag were identity documents, her driver's license, her diary, a make-up kit, a Sony Xperia Z3 handset, and her passport with her visa stamped in it.

Singing and speeches carried on until 2 a.m. Only close family members were left. Males slept in the bedrooms, and females slept in the lounge. TD slept on the floor. Her handbag was just by her head, two metres from an open window. Between 2 a.m. and 5 a.m., when everyone was fast asleep, something strange happened. It's hard to tell exactly what took place. Once TD got up at 5 a.m., she checked for her handbag. It was missing from the floor near her head. Who could have come so close to TD's head to grab the handbag? Had a burglar come to the window and used a long wire, rod, or stick to fish out this handbag? What happened? Was it a case of divine intervention?

TD was accompanied by Mr and Mrs Nhamoinesu's son Francis to the nearest police station to make a report. The police wrote up the report and gave copy to TD. One officer accompanied TD and Francis to the house to check the scene of the incident and to do a search of the people around. Most people had already left for Gokwe, that is Neddie's home, to make funeral arrangements. The police officer could not search the rooms, so he went away.

TD was picked up by her son-in-law Dr Munyaradzi, who had been waiting for her all morning. It was now ten o'clock. She was running late to get to the Nyaradzo funeral parlour to identify her mother's body before it went for post-mortem. By 3 p.m., the family had their burial order and all the procedures had been completed. So TD was accompanied by her sister-in-law Divine and her cousin sister Neddie to the registrar in Harare to get originals of TD's birth certificate and marriage certificate. She was going to use these after the funeral to get new identity documents, a new passport, and a new visa to return to the UK. TD was asked to collect those two documents the following morning at ten o'clock.

TD stayed at her daughter's as everyone else returned to Mainway Meadows, the venue for the mourners. The following day, Dr Careen and TD picked up the documents and went to the funeral parlour to identify Neddie's body, which was ready for transfer to Gokwe. TD's sister Dorothea was busy with buying flowers and lace for their mum. The bus was waiting to transport mourners to Gokwe. By 2 p.m. everyone was on their way to Gokwe, accompanying Neddie's body to her final resting place.

After the burial, and with all the necessary procedures done, TD and her daughter left for Gweru to get a new identity card. The following day, they left for the Harare passport office. TD applied for a new passport, which was be ready in four days. With the help of her daughter, she applied for a visa online, and submitted a copy of her application form, her passport, and all her supporting documents to FedEx to be sent to British Embassy agents in Harare. These were sent to the British Embassy in Pretoria, South Africa.

The following day TD was on her way to Gokwe to be with her father. Her siblings were still there. She comforted her father and consoled him during this most difficult time. After some time, all her siblings flew back except her young brother Izwi. TD and Izwi carried on being by their father's side, helping him cope with the loss.

According to TD, it was part of God's plan that her handbag had disappeared. TD continually showed no worry over the loss. She informed everyone who asked her about the stolen passport that it was God's plan. It would have been a disaster to go away and leave their father in that circumstance. God knew that Neddie's death was going to spark controversy. For the unveiling of events after Neddie was gone, knowledgeable advisors needed to be around Lazarus, as per God's plan. The Diocese of Central Zimbabwe was the sore point for Lazarus after his wife passed away. He could have suffered a stroke and died straight after his wife's death. But Sister Phoebe, TD and Izwi stood as potential counsellors, as did the well-wishers who were visiting or phoning to share a word of comfort with him. Newspapers ran headlines reading, "Clergy buries wife in church", which was uninformed news indicating a proper lack of knowledge of God and how he was working at Gokwe. On 29 November 2016, Radio Zimbabwe Station (ZBC) had a two-hour phone-in session, during which it became clear that the public needed education and more enlightenment about the work of God in Gokwe. In a statement made in January 2017, the diocese disassociated itself from the practice of burying a person inside a church. The diocese asked the Gokwe Town Council to address the matter, but according to hearsay, the council said that according to its by-laws, it had no case against Reverend Canon Muyambi. On 9 December 2016, the *New Zimbabwe* published an article reporting that the diocese was totally against Lazarus's having buried his wife in the church. Apparently the diocese said that Neddie could be exhumed from the grave and buried somewhere else in order to comply with Central Zimbabwe Diocese tradition. There was no way of blocking these false newspaper reports. All this hearsay reached Lazarus's ears, filtering in slowly, as his advisors did not want to pile too much of this bad news on him.

In January 2016, Reverend John Makiwa, who is Reverend Lazarus's right-hand man at the Healing Centre, had his license revoked by the diocese. Reverend Makiwa is also a chaplain for the primary school, the secondary school, and the convent of the CZM, and he ministers to two out-stations. This was a big blow, not only to John, Lazarus, and his family, but also to one thousand primary schoolchildren, three hundred secondary schoolchildren, twenty-six orphans, and twenty-five nuns. Was this decision a godly one?

On 25 December 2016, St Agnes Church was locked per the bishop's instruction. The parishioners were informed to leave and to worship somewhere else, such as in a classroom or under a tree. This was another big blow. One would imagine that when two bulls are fighting in an open field, one is defeated and runs away. We were very optimistic that one was going to run away as the loser, so it did happen. Reverend Lazarus and Neddie had built this church years ago in a place where all other priests had failed. Bishop Mark Wood had asked Reverend Lazarus to go and fight the darkness in Gokwe and to establish a vibrant parish, because all the priests he had sent had met with challenges.

In any event, Izwi and TD remained at Reverend Lazarus's side, talking him through these problems, and Sister Phoebe was constantly checking on his blood sugar level and blood pressure. Amidst all this, Lazarus remained silent and in prayer. A friend in need is a friend indeed.

All being well, TD could have travelled to the UK on 12 December 2016, but God said no. She was optimistic that God had some business for her at Gokwe. TD's son has family in Gweru, and her daughter has family in Harare. She could have stayed with them, but she felt God had business with her at Gokwe. She returned to the UK on 20 January 2017 after being satisfied that her father was stable. His blood sugar and blood pressure levels were good. He seemed to be coping with the situation. The dust seemed to have settled. Schools had just opened, and every department seemed to be running well.

During this period when TD was in Zimbabwe, she wrote a book about Irene Neddie. It kept her very busy, as she spoke to different people gathering relevant information. Her brother Izwi was very busy with administration issues for all of his father's projects, which are as follows:

- the St Agnes Children's Home
- the CZM Primary School
- the Logos Girls' High School
- the Health and Healing Medical Clinic.

Izwi was moving from office to office at Gokwe Town Centre, making sure that all outstanding issues were resolved and that everything was in place. He supervised the erection of a security fence around all Muyambi Village projects to make sure students and residents at the Centre were safeguarded and assured of security. One entrance to the Centre was put in place. A security guard shelter was constructed at the gate, and security officers were there twenty-four hours a day to monitor the coming in and going out of people and traffic. This gave a sense of security and belonging to everyone at the Centre. Because the soil was eroding, Izwi made sure all roads had gravel put on them for easy access to all departments. Reverend Lazarus felt pride and joy in having such a supportive family. It was very consoling. Izwi and TD addressed schoolchildren, teachers, and nuns to encourage them, reassure them, and strengthen them.

Izwi finally had meetings with two bishops, one of whom being Bishop Ishmael Mukuwanda. This meeting, which was on 12 January 2017 at 11.30 a.m. at the Diocese of Central Zimbabwe offices, was meant to seek clarification on the letter that Reverend Mazula had read to the congregation at St Agnes Parish on 25 December 2016, a service that TD had attended, and a letter the bishop had written to Reverend Lazarus dated 1 January 2017. Some of the outcomes of this first meeting lifted Reverend John Makiwa's suspension from offering the seven sacraments at Reverend Lazarus's properties. The bishop also asked that Reverend Muyambi provide a calendar of when the bishop's services would be required at Gokwe. It was also agreed that the St

Agnes Church, which the bishop had instructed to be locked, should be open to the public if they wanted to use it for individual prayers.

The bishop had had the church locked as a tactic to solve pending issues at the time and to allow dust to settle, as there was division within the congregation. It is said that on the day the church was closed, some people, like Mrs Kambanga and Mrs Kapembeza, sobbed bitterly in private. No one had expected this move, but they had to adhere to the rule for the purpose of peace. This issue had been prophesied some time back: if Lazarus and Neddie did not pray very hard, then the church would be closed one day. But they could have forgotten about the prophecy. The prophecy was fulfilled soon after Neddie's death. Neddie had also spoken about this day before her death (see her conversation with Rhodah Cynthia Madovi).

Izwi finally flew back to the United Kingdom on 13 January 2017. Reverend Lazarus felt a great relief after this, but the battle appeared still to be on. He received the news that Mr Uta, a dedicated supporter of the work at Gokwe and of all of Reverend Muyambi's projects, a Loving and Caring Member of the Zimbabwe Healing Centre, and a supplier of one of the security guards at Reverend Lazarus's Healing Centre, had been suspended from attending two consecutive standing committee meetings at the diocesan office. The reason was not known at that time.

TD carried on supporting her father spiritually as they prayed together. She supported him physically as she had sessions of physical exercise with him, sometimes allowing the eighty-three-year-old men to run. Reverend Lazarus is naturally active and does exercises by himself to keep fit. He has a gymnastic bicycle which he rides daily. Sister Phoebe continued to support Reverend Lazarus in the same way she had supported Lazarus and Neddie when Neddie was alive. Neddie had taught Sister Phoebe how to look after Lazarus as the former grew old and weak. Sister Phoebe was an asset, a pillar, a person to rely on in difficult times. She also needed cushioning, as it took a long time for her to come to terms with Neddie's departure from this word. A lot of negative things were said about Sister Phoebe's support of Neddie and Reverend Lazarus, but Neddie had advised that she should not listen to the world lest she fail to look after the founder and owner of CZM. Lazarus and Neddie's children supported Sister Phoebe and allowed her to carry on looking after their father, as she had all the required experience. She also had a good-paying job at Logos High School as manager. Her eldest brother, Mr T. Chakadayi, came to strengthen his sister amidst the speculations.

Since the inception of the CZM, Sister Phoebe was part of the third group of sisters who made their final life vows to serve God as nuns. She left family and all worldly passions and desires behind to work for God. She chose a selfless life, a sacrificial life, and a life devoted to God's service. She chose to marry Jesus instead of a human being. All her salary monies go to the CZM coffers as per her vows. She takes not one cent from it. The nuns share all they have as a family. Some nuns have violated their vows and taken control of their money, having fallen victim to the love of money and forgotten the vows they had taken. They have abandoned the other unemployed nuns who live on the convent budget. Those who have more money have opted to look after their families, something which could have been agreed to as a community, so that there would be money in the budget for everyone's family. That's what it means to be a nun. It's very sacrificial and not selfish.

Before Neddie passed away, she and Lazarus had asked Sister Phoebe to sleep at their home, because Lazarus's illness had become a big challenge. Neddie would sleep deeply sometimes, so at times she even asked Sister Phoebe to sleep in the same bedroom with them so the latter could attend to Lazarus. All was done with Sister Phoebe's consent. She became a very helpful asset at a time when help was needed. The entire family appreciated her. These are Sister Phoebe's words:

> My life is nothing without God and Jesus as my personal Saviour. I have sacrificed everything to work for God as a nun. I have left all to follow Jesus and have not turned back. The founder and owner of CZM is Reverend Lazarus and the late Irene Neddie Muyambi. They did it [founded the CZM] when the diocese was not in support of it. They got no help but used their money to make sure we were happy. They are our parents, and we cannot abandon them in their old age. We are here because they have loved us, accepted us, and allowed us to live in their house initially before a convent was built, because the diocese had said

they should take full responsibility for their independent religious community. So if we can't look after them and their vision, whether they are alive or dead, what does God say about us? God must be unhappy. I have vowed to look after them till death do us part. I know my reward is in heaven. I shall continue to hold on to what I am holding, for it will give me rewards. I shall continue to run this race set before me until I receive my crown. I can have flaws, but I am human and I pray for perfection every day, for I don't want to miss my crown.

Great words from Sister Phoebe. In such difficult times, you see who is on your side and who is not. But God has taught us to love everybody as he has loved us, irrespective of our sinful nature.

If TD and Izwi had returned to the UK, leaving their father to face all these challenges by himself, it would not have been right in God's eyes. That's probably why TD's return was delayed. She strongly believes God stopped her from going back. She said, "There is always a reason for everything that happens in our lives. God has business with me in Gokwe. If I do not obey, I will suffer like Jonah, who spent three days in the belly of a fish. Even if my visa is out, I shall not rush to go back to the UK. I will wait for my father and God himself to release me. I have so much to document about the death of my mother and the aftermath of her death. This is history. Someone should document it. God has chosen me to do it because he knows I have had passion for writing books from since the time I was a member of the Budding Writers Association of Zimbabwe years ago, and from the time I wrote my first book on the work at the Zimbabwe Healing Centre, Gokwe."

After the British Embassy refused to give TD a visa, citing that she had not provided enough information, for instance evidence that she had left the UK on 21 November 2016 when her mother died, TD appealed online to the British Embassy in Pretoria, providing evidence of the airline ticket she had used to travel to Zimbabwe. Her vicar, Reverend Susan Barter, of St Paul's Church in Bordesley Green, Birmingham, UK, had to get involved. She felt compelled to help her parishioner who was in great need.

As far as TD was concerned, God had caused the delay because she had an indefinite leave to remain in the UK and as far as she was concerned, there was no need for the embassy refusal to just issue copy. TD remained at Gokwe waiting for her visa. For sure she was a comforter and consoler in her father's time of need. Even after she got her visa, she stayed about two weeks more, until she was sure Lazarus and God had set her free.

One other strange thing was that for TD to get a new passport and visa and to change travelling dates with the airline, it would cost about $1,503 in total. TD was on unpaid leave at work, so her vicar and members of the Diocese of Birmingham Mothers' Union helped financially. One of the members asked her husband to go and deposit £150 in TD's bank account, and he mistakenly added another zero. Instead, £1,500 was credited to TD's account. The couple did not ask for an immediate refund, but they did ask TD to repay the difference in instalments when she got back to work. How wonderful some people are. How wonderful God is to his people. Is this not God at work? Is this not God making sure all was well for TD and her family? Neddie's death was sudden and unexpected, so TD just travelled with the little funds she had. What we should know is that if God puts you in a situation, he will see you through it (1 Corinthians 10:13). In Romans, Paul says, "All things work together for good to those who know God." In the book of Job, Job acknowledges that he has heard people speak of God working in their lives, and has seen with his own eyes God manifesting himself in his life. TD says she has become stronger through this incident and the death of her mother. She says she is at a heightened stage in her relationship with God.

If God cares for the flowers that bloom, if God cares for the rivers that flow, if God cares for the birds that sing, I know he will care also for his people, who are more important and who are created in his image. That is TD's faith. Her faith is unshaken and unwavering. She strengthened and reassured all who were in contact with her at Gokwe. She strengthened Reverend John Makiwa, who was hard hit at the time, grieving over Neddie's death. She encouraged everyone to remain solid in prayer. TD and all her siblings went on a ten-day fast from 9 January 2017 to 18 January 2017. Their prayer points were for the following:

- their mother's soul to rest in eternity
- their father to be strengthened mentally and physically
- their father's health to be restored so he could complete the tasks God had set before him
- the prosperity of their parents' independent projects within the Diocese of Central Zimbabwe.

The children stood solid and united behind their father and late mother. Those abroad kept phoning their father and reassuring him. They stood firm against the challenges which arose in the aftermath of their mother's death, equipping their father with all the necessary weapons of spiritual defence.

Looking back at why and how TD's journey was delayed, I conclude that it is simply a mystery. Thinking about that moment her handbag disappeared, one wonders if some divine intervention was at work that night. Her delayed return turned out to be for a good cause.

By Tinaye Matsveru

Orphans Mourn Neddie

I am an orphan. I was brought to St Agnes Children's Home in the year 2001 when I was four years old. I was just found straying and was taken to social services. I attended preschool, where Mrs Muyambi was my teacher. After graduating from preschool, I joined CZM Primary School. I repeated grade 1 in 2004. I repeated grade 6, and in 2012 I sat for my grade 7 examinations. I came out with twenty-seven units, and then I proceeded to Njelele Secondary School. In 2015, when I was in third form, I was transferred to Blue Hills Home in Gweru. In February of 2016, I ran away from Blue Hills and returned to St Agnes Children's Home. I was given a warm welcome by Reverend Lazarus and Mrs Muyambi. Sister Phoebe took me to social services and the police. In March I was removed and taken to Gokwe North to live with foster parents. I returned to Reverend and Mrs Muyambi because I was not happy anywhere else. I asked them to give me a job. They gave me one of their spare bedrooms to live, and work in their garden for a salary.

I want to thank my mother, Mrs Muyambi, for looking after me, and for giving me food and shelter and also money. I want to thank them for looking after orphans. This is where I call home.

—Thembelani Tapiwa Dube

• • • • • • • ● • • • • • • •

Mum had a good heart. Whatever we asked from her, she gave us. She taught us not to take anything without asking. Mum discouraged us from taking things without permission. She encouraged us to work hard at school so as to yield good results. She encouraged us to pray every day so as to avoid being used by the devil. Mum encouraged us to sing Hymn 130, "Mukristu Usanete", to read the Bible, and to pray. She treated us as her own children, and we never felt that we were orphaned. We had a mother who provided for our needs. We never struggled. She shared her resources with us whenever we ran out of food. She taught us to use our hands for survival. She taught us how to build, make bricks, and paint, stating that we cannot pay for everything. Our mum looked after us from the time she was changing our nappies as babies until the time she left us as grown-ups. Therefore, her death has hurt us so much. We did not know that God would take our mother who treated us so well. We did not expect it to happen. All young and old orphans were in tears, and so were our carers. We mourned together. It was very painful. We had never experienced such pain before for she was the only mother we'd known since we were babies. She loved us with all her heart. Mum, rest in peace.

—Grace, Moses, and Abednego, St Agnes Children's Home

Neddie Writes about the Building of St Agnes Area

During the month of June 1971 there came a letter from the bishop of Matabeleland asking us to leave Botswana and take a new post in Gokwe. We did not respond to this letter, so the bishop wrote a second letter asking us what we had decided to do. The biblical story of Jonah had a big influence on our decision-making process. We took up the post, filled with fear of the unknown. Gokwe had a reputation for malaria and tsetse flies. It was very remote and had been side lined as far as development was concerned.

That same year in October, the construction of the priest's house in Gokwe was started. We waited until early February, and then decided to leave Serowe in Botswana for Gokwe. We arrived in Bulawayo on 7 February 1972 with our personal property, which Mr Palmer helped us to transport using his lorry. My husband drove to Gokwe to check if the house was complete. He found that the house was only halfway finished. The bishop advised that we go home and wait until the house was complete. We did as he'd suggested.

My husband went to Gokwe again in March to check, but the house was not completed yet. We therefore stayed at our home in Wedza until the bishop sent a telegram on 8 May saying the house was complete and that all the property had been sent to Gokwe.

On 13 May Lazarus and I left our homeland, Wedza, to live in Gokwe. The first Sunday, which was the fourteenth, we had our own service with our children. Later, one woman came to check if the priest had arrived. The first challenge we faced was water. We had to walk two miles to and from the borehole. This means that each day we walked four miles to fetch enough water for our household needs. The following Friday, my husband went to the nearest school, Gokwe School, for the right of entry. When he was there, he met a man called Mambwere who knew a man who could find us a place to dig a well. Mr Mambwere brought Mr Materekeshe, a person who could locate underground sources of water. The first place was twenty feet from the house, and the other was thirty feet from the house. He went away, and later brought three men, who dug the well. In four days they had reached twenty-one feet and water was coming out. They started building the wall of the well from the bottom using stone and cement. When they had finished building, they dug the well five feet deeper. Yet more water was coming out. On 15 June 1972 the well was completed.

The next task to tackle was the building of the office and the bishop's rondavels. Mr Hlekisani, who had built the rectory, was asked to build the two structures. As he moulded the bricks, my husband was organising how he was going to build the church. Mr Hlekisani started building the bishop's and office rondavels. On 12 September, two builders came on a mission to start building the church. These were Mr Marufu and Mr Chikura. The bishop visited on 23 September and found that the corners of the church building were already raised. The people of Gokwe were busy making bricks in turns. Those who lived far away had to send in some money for help. One of the builders, Mr Marufu, lost a relative, so he went to Selukwe. He never came back again. My husband continued to struggle to get people to help with the building. The other builder volunteered his time to St Agnes and carried on to complete the job. In early December, the walls of the church were complete. Now there was the roofing problem. The priest went here and there and tried this and that to get the roofing material. The priest, my husband, went to Kwekwe, called Reverend Haynes, and met Mr Marufu, who worked for ZISCO. They had a meeting to discuss the roofing matter. The ZISCO manager was a member of the Anglican Church, so he provided the roofing material free of charge to my husband. Mr Mloyi was asked to make holes in the roofing material so it would fit properly. Mr Musa, the manager of Gokwe Supply Stores, helped by transporting the roofing material from Kwekwe to St Agnes in Gokwe for free. He looked for someone to put the roof, finding that it would be very expensive. In early February 1974, my husband and other men organised themselves and fitted the roof on a Saturday. My husband was assisted by Mr Munyoro, Mr Mapurisa, Mr Murehwa, and the builder who fitted the roof on no expense, seeing the trouble that my husband was going through.

Now that the big job was complete, the builder was now busy on the walls, while others fitted windowpanes and painted the walls. The builder built the altar and finished up the floor. My husband was speeding up the whole job now. On the day the baptism pond was completed and painted, the bishop arrived to dedicate the church building. The spirit and cooperation shown during the building was unheard of. I had not seen such a spirit of unity. I am sure God was with them. Men and women, boys and girls, worked together.

The dedication of the church building was a big day. A big beast was slaughtered. People ate sadza and drank mahewu. There was no beer provided for the sake of peace and discipline. People of all different denominations were there to witness the occasion. The church was full up to the extent that other people stood outside. I was teaching at Gokwe School at the time, so the senior and junior choirs sang. Those gathered ate and chatted joyfully. The following day, the bishop confirmed the building and said the first Mass in the new church.

I thank Christians near and far who lent a hand to this work of building the church. I thank our children, who were deprived of support sometimes as we put our physical and financial support towards getting the job done, for their patience.

We started another project of building a church at St James the Great Nyamuroro at Nembudziya, Gokwe.

—N. Irene Muyambi

Neddie's Life in Botswana (1970–1972)

After my husband had been transferred from Hwange in Rhodesia to Serowe in Botswana, we settled well.

I had been in Botswana for five months, stationed at St Augustine Parish in Serowe. After two months of my staying in Serowe, there came a letter from the Mothers' Union (MU) president asking for a presiding member for each district. The letter was handed to the enrolling member, and she addressed her members to see if anyone was willing and free to take up that role. They could not get anyone to be the presiding member, so I offered to do the job for the period I was going to be in Botswana.

I started my work as a presiding member towards the end of July. The first branches I visited were Shoshong and Mahalapye. St Faith's Church in Shoshong had three full members only, and I had to approach two new members who were willing to join. They paid their membership fees. They did not meet for MU prayers because they thought their number too few.

At St James's Church Mahalapye, the mothers were not organised, and finding a meeting place for prayers was a big challenge. They were not meeting for prayers. I spoke to some of the mothers who were willing to join the MU. I asked one of the women to visit members in their homes and talk to them about the MU. We managed to enrol seven, so all in all there were thirteen paid-up members. At St Cyprian Church in Selika, I mobilised the women and opened a new branch. At St Augustine Parish, where my husband was the priest in charge, six members were meeting for MU since I had joined them at the end of March. In this branch only elderly mothers were members. Young mothers only came to church on Sunday. The MU met on Fridays in the afternoon. They said prayers and swept the church. The MU timetable was not followed. The priest had never been invited to address them. The MU members were good at raising money and welcoming visitors, but on the spiritual side they were lacking. New members could join if the timetable was followed so as to make the movement interactive and attractive.

—Irene Neddie Muyambi

Neddie Writes about Mothers' Union and the St Agnes Guild in Gokwe (1979)

There are thirteen Mothers' Union (MU) branches which I started since arriving in Gokwe from Botswana in 1972. I have visited twelve of them twice. We observe the wave of prayer and the Lady Day. We also have training days.

Eight girls have been enrolled for the St Agnes Guild. We have a big gathering in September, at which time thirty girls will be enrolled.

The MU members and the guild help in the healing ministry. They support the sick and needy people, as they understand our work in Gokwe. They also take care of the church building, washing vestments and cleaning inside and outside the church.

—Irene Neddie Muyambi

• • • • • • • • • ● • • • • • • • • • •

The author looked at the paperwork on MU meetings at St Agnes Parish. Neddie used to run MU quiet days, during which time members would receive teachings on different topics. Some of the teachings Neddie provided were on the following:
- the seven Catholic sacraments
- the establishment of the MU in 1876 by Mary Sumner
- family relationships
- money
- children
- relatives

- visiting the bereaved
- disobedience
- infertility
- HIV/AIDS
- acts of mercy
- pastoral care.

If this book were to include Neddie's teachings on the above topics, then a thick volume would be produced.

Neddie's desire to take Mothers' Union forward was based on the vision of Mothers' Union to see a world where God's love is shown through loving, respectful, and flourishing relationships.

Irene understood the aim and purpose of Mothers' Union to demonstrate the Christian faith by way of action through the transformation of communities worldwide by nurturing the family in its many forms. She knew her role in upholding Christ's teaching on the nature of marriage and in promoting its wider understanding. Irene knew her responsibility as set by MU objectives, to encourage parents to bring up their children in the faith and life of the church and to maintain a worldwide fellowship of Christians united in prayer, worship, and service.

She was a champion in promoting conditions in society favourable to stable family life and the protection of children, and in helping those whose family life had met with adversity. It is wonderful to see how Mothers' Union has over the years strived for a better society, and to see how people like Neddie have raised its flag without wavering.

Father Muyambi Reflecting in 1997 (Taken from His Archives)

From the time I left Botswana on 14 May 1972, after being asked by Bishop Mark Wood to go and challenge Gokwe, I have definitely challenged Gokwe.

The St Agnes Church Parish

The church of St Agnes Parish is growing, and the work of the gospel is progressing well. There is even a plan to construct or extend the existing church building, which is turning out to be too small. As the mother church in Gokwe, after Bishop Mark Wood had assisted in the construction of St Luke's Church at Mateta and St James's Church at Nyamuroro, St Agnes planted other church buildings, namely St Michael's at Manoti, Marondamashanu at Gumunyu, and St Barnabas at Empress Mine.

Still on the development of the gospel, I supervised the planting of four other church buildings: Church of Christ the Healer at Simchembo, St David at Nyaradzo, St Barnabas at Makore, and St Francis at Ganyungu. This is highly recommended as hard work which is being done in Gokwe through community participation.

My vision is still furthering to the extension of a mission at Zhombe Growth Point in Chief Nenyunga's area and at Nembudziya Mutora Growth Point. The community can provide or assist in most physical duties like brick moulding and building, and do other outstanding activities.

Within the St Agnes Parish there are other departments, like the Zimbabwe Spiritual Health and Healing Centre W.O. 17/79, the St Agnes Gokwe Children's Home C.R. 772, the Community of Chita cheZvipo zveMoto, and the Convent of Chita cheZvipo zveMoto primary school, crèche, and preschool.

The Zimbabwe Spiritual Healing and Manger Centre deals with attending to the sick, work which is assisted by the Holy Spirit (messengers from the Lord) during the time of Prisca Marumirofa. The work is still going on. The healing team, which is under my leadership, helps the sick and suffering. I am sometimes invited to haunted schools, clinics, and other churches within and outside the Diocese of Central Zimbabwe to help with exorcism.

The voice of the Lord is still actively assisting in the work. The Centre is being extended. There is already an approved clinic, and there are two dormitories which are to be completed.

St Agnes Gokwe Children's Home C.R. 772

The home, which started giving care to the orphaned children in 1980, is still doing the good work. At the moment there are forty-eight children in the home. Most of these children are those whose mothers would have died post-delivery. The children come mostly from within the two districts of Gokwe, North and South, and a few others from the districts within the Midlands province.

The Community of Chita cheZvipo zveMoto (CZM)

The community is made up of nuns and friars. The following is a breakdown of how many they are at the moment.

Final life vow	13
Junior profession	6
Novices	9
Postulants	2
Aspirants	3
Associates	2

Total   35

The members are increasing in number. Educationally they are progressing to secondary education. Some are already qualified teachers, nurses, and builders. Some also work hard in the fields to earn a happy living.

With regard to farming, there is

- cattle rearing;
- poultry keeping;
- gardening;
- crop growing;
- orchard tending; and
- goat rearing.

All this is meant for consumption and income generation.

The school we opened is catering for our orphans and the surrounding community. It is three years old and doing well. Last year, 1996, the pupils competed in music at the provincial level. They have been number 1 and 2 at the zone and district levels.

Furthermore, there is a school for the blind. At the moment there are seven blind pupils. These are directly being cared for by my wife, Neddie. I am responsible for their feeding. They definitely need financial support.

It is quite a challenging job at the Centre, but it is benefitting the growth of God's kingdom.

—Reverend Canon Lazarus Tashaya Muyambi

Prisca Marumirofa Is Visited by an Angel (Written by Neddie; Taken from Her Archives)

This girl fell ill in November of 1976. Her whole body was shaking. She had been in hospital for some time. On 24 December, her illness intensified. Her chest felt as though it were air-filled, like a balloon. Feeling like it would explode, she stayed awake all night.

On 25 December around 9 a.m., Prisca was left with her mum at home while everyone else had gone to church. She had a dream/vision in which she saw someone dressed in white/silver clothing coming eastwards from heaven. This messenger held a red book. He landed on the outskirts of the homestead and then walked towards the homestead. When he got to the house, he called, "Prisca!" Prisca answered, "Father." This messenger entered the house where Prisca was sleeping and said, "Prisca, wake up and let us pray." They prayed together. After the prayer, this messenger started to teach her how to sing church songs. One of the songs was "Mufudzi Unondida", which is Hymn 111 in the Anglican Prayer Book.

While this was going on, Prisca's mother was outside. When she heard the singing, she entered the house and asked her daughter what was going on. Prisca explained everything to her mother. Meanwhile this messenger was kneeling by Prisca's legs. Prisca saw him, but her mother could not see the messenger. When her mother left the room, Prisca carried on singing. Prisca's mother returned to enquire, but Prisca informed her that she must not worry, saying she was being taught to pray and sing. Therefore she asked her mother not to disturb the messenger. Prisca's mother ran to church to inform her husband. Upon their return, Prisca explained to her father what had happened. He ran back to church and informed everyone. After church, everyone went to Prisca's home to hear and see this surprise visitor from heaven. After hearing the story, they prayed and went away.

During sunset Prisca started teaching the villagers about what the messenger had instructed her to tell them. On 26 December, she called for the villagers to gather. When they had gathered, Prisca started speaking powerfully and knowledgeably. The messenger was speaking through her. The parents were advised to take Prisca to Gokwe Centre to Reverend Muyambi so he could lay hands upon her, so that the Holy Spirit would be bestowed on her and allow her to start God's work. On 28 December, the family brought Prisca to St Agnes Parish, to Lazarus. She was brought in an ox-driven cart. Reverend Lazarus and wife Neddie went to meet them by car after receiving the message that they were on their way to the mission. Reverend and Mrs Muyambi brought them to the mission. Prisca was accompanied by her father and uncle. We went straight in to St Agnes Church and prayed. Prisca's father explained everything that had transpired. They gave the messenger time to talk and explain to them who he was and for what purpose he had been sent. The messenger introduced himself as Archangel Michael. In his words through Prisca, he said that people should turn away from evil deeds, serve God, and stop worshipping other gods. Furthermore, he mentioned that when Prisca felt air in her chest, it was the angel healing her and removing every ailment.

The angel informed them that their faith was the way to and the light of heaven. People need to cultivate their hearts so they can be clean, and should stop pleasing the devil. Most people are the devil's seed, and they please the devil more than God. If the devil is shaking us, we ought to shake the devil. People worship God and other gods, and they seek the pleasures of the world to gratify their flesh instead of gratifying the Spirit.

This angel stayed at Gokwe for three months teaching before he departed for heaven. On the day he left, everyone was upset. He had been a good company.

• • • • • • • • • ● • • • • • • • • •

Comment

Looking at Neddie's narrative, I find it strange that she welcomed this girl to live with her in her house, providing food, clothing, and shelter. Truly she had great faith, and a big heart. She even drove to meet Prisca. She believed it was God speaking through Prisca. She believed the angel was from God. Her faith was immeasurable.

Neddie welcomed the poorest in her house. I wonder where Neddie is right now. According to Matthew 25:35, strangers are to be welcomed, fed, clothed, and housed. If Jesus's definition of a stranger is as it seems, then as we welcome the less privileged, we also welcome Jesus.

Neddie was comfortable with not only those who spoke her language or who were teachers like her, but also with all people created by God. She was a miracle. Mother Teresa had opposition from her own religious community, but she fought for what she knew. Neddie fought for what she believed in and humbled herself just to demonstrate her relationship with God.

Rest in peace, our mother.

Neddie's Life, CZM inception and uniform: by Sister Phoebe (CZM)

The idea of the Community of the Holy Fire (CZM) uniform came about when Reverend Lazarus consulted the holy angels asking how to design the uniform. He was advised to invite Mrs Mutani from the Diocese of Manicaland, Mrs Nyati from the Diocese of Matabeleland, and Mrs Muyambi. These clergy wives came together and were taught how to design the uniform, which was a grey dress with red stars. The same design scheme applied to the uniform for the founders, Lazarus and Neddie, although theirs one included a hat of the same colours. Lazarus's uniform had seven red stars, representing the seven gifts.

At the inception of the CZM, Neddie would give some of her clothes to the nuns, as they did not have enough clothes. Before the nuns had working habits, Neddie provided them with clothes, compromising her own family to do so.

As years went by, when a nun fell ill or passed on, Neddie looked beyond CZM divisional barriers and visited each one of them. This was made possible by the financial help from her adult children. She remained their mother until death did them part. Even some of the nuns' family members, for instance parents, were amongst those for whom Neddie cared at the Healing Centre until they died. She was an expert at providing end-of-life or palliative care.

Neddie did the same for her in-laws. She brought her husband's family members to the Healing Centre, keeping them in her house until point of death.

At the inception of the orphanage, Neddie used her bed sheets to make baby napkins. She donated soap, clothes, Vaseline, milk, and other items using her own money.

As years went by, she became the deputy superintendent of the orphanage. She worked extra hard to source food, clothes, toys, and money from people she knew, including family, from all over the country and beyond the borders. She never gave up, not even at the time when Zimbabwe was hard hit economically. She continually strived to support those in need.

Neddie had so much love for nuns and orphans, treating them as her own children. As an experienced mother, she taught the nuns how to care for babies. Whenever Reverend Lazarus was away, Neddie had to drive the orphans or sick people to hospital as per their need.

During her ministry, she travelled and taught the Christian way of life as written in the book of James. She taught others to look after orphans and widows. At the time when she was Mothers' Union coordinator for Gokwe North and South, she travelled, sometimes on foot, to meet MU members, fitting in with them as one of them. The people from the twenty outstations received a lot of material and moral and spiritual help from Neddie. She never wanted her position to be felt or her economic status to influence the way she dealt with anyone. She was down to earth.

From this description of Neddie, it is clear that the way to heaven is to be worked for and the Christian life is a race that needs to be won through hard work. As one runs the race, one need not to be turning back. Just run towards your goal, because your crown awaits you. I want to believe that Neddie has attained her crown.

The Bible says that if anyone wants to be a leader amongst others, he must be like a little child (Matthew 18:1–5). We are encouraged to be more servants than masters in our leadership roles. To follow Christ we need to deny ourselves, take up the cross, and follow Jesus. No one who puts her hand on the plough and turns back is fit for the kingdom of heaven. It is evidently clear that Neddie did not turn back after putting her hand to the plough. She kept herself busy in God's field.

People's Dreams about Neddie

Mrs Caroline Mazula dreamt of seeing Neddie Muyambi dressed in dazzling white and silver clothes. She was coming from the St Agnes Rectory. Mrs Mazula and Mrs Dorothea Matsveru were walking from the St Agnes Parish church. When they got close to Neddie, they tried to greet her, but she greeted them with her fingertips and disappeared from them, going eastwards.

Mrs Tholanah dreamt of Neddie dressed in her Mothers' Union uniform. It was new, bright-coloured, and outstanding. She looked fit and strong. She was holding a fifty-kilogram sack with just a cupful measurement of groundnuts in a corner. She asked Mrs Tholanah if her groundnuts were sown in her field, for she wanted them sown. She asked if they were sown as in all the other years. Mrs Tholanah informed her that she did not know where the seeds for the groundnuts were. Neddie said that Mrs Tholanah should not worry, for she knew who had taken her groundnuts. She also said she was coming to take the hero home, pointing at her husband, who was sitting in a chair. She sang the song "Iva Gamba Utarise Mhandu" ("Be a Hero and Face the Enemy"). She also sang "Soja Kumusha" ("Soldier, Go Home") as she disappeared from Mrs Tholanah's sight.

Mercy Chirimuuta dreamt of a large herd of cattle and one pig. She saw Mrs Maromo coming from the rubbish pit. The pig wanted to attack her, so she asked Mrs Maromo to walk fast. Mrs Maromo came in through the gate. The cattle changed into pigs, so there were now many pigs. Mercy sat next to the gate, and one pig came to attack her. She attacked back, pushing its head into its body. She then saw many people coming. Ahead of them was a police officer with a baton. The police officer was saying he wanted to see where Mrs Muyambi was buried. He also wanted to know what was so special about her that she was buried in church. Who was she? He wanted to exhume her. Mercy Chirimuuta wanted to get out of the orphanage because they were opening all the doors, looking for Mrs Muyambi's grave. When she went out, it was dazzling bright. She then saw Mrs Muyambi with a dazzling face. It was so bright that she could not face her brightness. Mrs Muyambi said, "Mercy, have these people been here before?" She said she didn't know.

One of the orphans, Admire, replied, "Yes, they have been here before."

Mrs Muyambi said, "Don't show them where I was buried, because something will happen."

Vela dreamt of Neddie wearing her Mothers' Union uniform which shone so bright and beautiful. She was standing near Vela. They were both watching a gathering of Mothers' Union women. Amongst them was Neddie's daughter Dorothea. Neddie pointed to the gathering and said to Vela, "That is my firstborn child." Neddie then walked towards Dorothea and gave her a big hug.

PART II

The Aftermath of Neddie's Departure

Neddie's dream and vision was to see Mothers' Union flourish to the point of building a dining hall, kitchen, office, and library at St Agnes Parish. Writing in 1996, Neddie said, "We are a union of forty-eight mothers who meet Thursdays and Saturdays. We plan our programme in intervals three months in duration. One of our activities is a monthly address by the priest in charge, Reverend Canon L. T. Muyambi. We have a yearly conference where we meet all members in the diocese. As a way of expressing devotion in preparation for days like Christmas, we plan for quiet days for all members in the mission district. We also observe Lady Day yearly. Acts of love are expressed in deeds, like a monthly donation to the orphanage. We visit the sick, the aged, and backsliders. One of our major objectives is to build a training centre where we can hold courses to train our mothers in basketry, cookery, dressmaking, pottery, etc. The centre can be used for hiring and fundraising activities. As mothers, we care and express love in a motherly way."

Unfortunately, Neddie retired before achieving her dreams. New priests in charge came to Gokwe to carry on where Lazarus and Irene Neddie had left off.

· · · · · · · · ● · · · · · · · · · ·

On Saturday, 19 November 2016, it was reported by Sister Phoebe (CZM) that, around seven o'clock in the evening, Neddie asked her husband what the position was of the title deeds for the projects they had tirelessly worked for over the years. In response Lazarus had said,

"Let us pray." After prayers, they spoke about it. It is said that two years back this couple had paid over $3,000 to Gokwe Town Council for the release of their title deeds, but it was been clear why they were not being given their title deeds.

The untimely death of Irene came when the bishops and their wives were at a conference in Malawi. Neddie's burial had to be pushed to Saturday, 26 November, so as to wait for Bishop Ishmael Mukuwanda's arrival. Lazarus chose Reverend Gwese of the Diocese of Harare to lead the funeral service for his wife. He chose Reverend Ncube of the Diocese of Matabeleland to bury his wife.

The St Agnes Church building was closed and locked, with parishioners asked to find an alternative place of worship in a hall or a classroom. On 20 November, after Neddie had received her last Holy Communion before her death, she rested by the orphanage and mentioned to Cynthia Madovi that there had been a prophecy that if Neddie and Lazarus did not pray hard, the church was going to be locked one day. This prophecy had now been fulfilled in everybody's eyes. It is against this backdrop that the author of this book has seen fit to include in this book an account of the aftermath of Neddie's departure from this world.

I hope this is going to help the Zimbabwean community and those over the borders to have a better understanding of the events surrounding Neddie's burial.

The events following Irene Neddie's departure are as follows:

A couple of days after Neddie's burial at the Trinity Chapel, a Zimbabwe Republic police officer arrived at Tashaya Residence, which was Neddie's home. He came at 9 p.m. to talk to Reverend Honorary Canon Muyambi. He stated that he had been sent by the Midlands Provincial Police Headquarters to investigate the issue of Neddie's burial in the church. The police officer was given all the information he required. He was also given a book, *Christian Healing Mission in Gokwe, Zimbabwe: A Success Story*, which is about the works that Irene Neddie had done alongside her husband. These works were the reason why she deserved the honour she was given.

On 8 November 2016, Reverend Lazarus had visitors from Nyaradzo Funeral Services, who had provided the services related to Neddie's burial. They had come to apologise for the way their employee, a bus driver, had misinformed the public using the WhatsApp social network to impart the information that Neddie had been buried in a church, when really it was a private independent chapel. These visitors also apologised for the adverse comments written about Lazarus by the bus driver during their latter's WhatsApp conversations with the public. The family appreciated their coming.

The story of Neddie's burial on 26 November 2016 raised a lot of eyebrows. People wondered why she was buried in a church. Obviously, the public was ignorant of the fact that it was a private chapel. They also were unaware of Neddie's achievements. The news came out on Zimbabwe Radio, the *Chronicle*, *Newsday*, the *Switzerland News*, Facebook, the *Zimbabwe News*, the *Zimbabwe Eye*, *Kwayedza*, and many other media and social media platforms. On top of this, the diocese issued a press statement. On Zimbabwe Radio, members of the public were phoning in and giving their opinions about how and why Neddie had been buried in a chapel, and why Reverend Honorary Canon Lazarus Muyambi and family had given Neddie that honour. It was clear that the public was misinformed and very ignorant of God's work in Gokwe. They were not aware that Neddie was buried in her own private chapel which she had built for God's service, a chapel she had built with her husband to serve the sick, the needy, and the suffering people of Gokwe, a chapel which also caters for all denominations. People from all walks of life visit this place seeking help. Neddie extended her helping hand to all. Her love went above religion, sexuality, racial barriers, economic status, and any other social lines.

The decision to bury Neddie in a chapel was embraced by everyone who had been in contact with Neddie in one way or another. This type of practice was not a new thing in the Anglican Catholic Church. The acting priest in charge, Reverend Mazula, and Reverend Gwese of Harare Diocese were the celebrants. Reverend John Makiwa of the Diocese of Central Zimbabwe and Reverend Ncube of the Diocese of Matabeleland laid Neddie to rest. This was a fair distribution of responsibilities for the burial of a woman like Neddie who was neither rich nor poor, neither great nor small. The bishop was in See, and preached at the funeral service, where he showered praises upon Neddie for the work she had done in the diocese, especially in the Mothers' Union, where she was very popular. Who did not know Neddie in the Diocese of Central Zimbabwe? Who in the diocese did not know that Neddie looked after orphans and the sick?

Also present at the funeral service was Bishop Flora of the Roman Catholic Diocese of Gokwe, with the company of priests and nuns. Bishop Flora spoke well of Neddie and said he had known her and her husband since 1974. He spoke about their commitment to God's work. During his speech, he referred to Neddie as a woman of substance and a woman of valour.

Different denominations were well represented at the funeral.

Well after the burial, people continued to flock Tashaya Residence to give their condolences to Reverend Lazarus. One of these people was Bishop Chad Gandiya of the Diocese of Harare, who came along with his wife. They visited the tomb in the chapel and expressed their appreciation of the honour bestowed upon this gracious woman, a woman of noble character. The tomb was well floored and polished such that one cannot tell there is a tomb there. Church services continue as usual.

After speaking to several people about this chapel burial, I decided to include the two following narratives, one of Sister Itayi of St James's Nyamandhlovu, Zimbabwe, and the other of Anesu Muyambi of Birmingham in the United Kingdom, taking a deeper look into church burials.

Sister Itayi (CZM) Speaks of Neddie

Sister Itayi (CZM) describes Mrs I. N. Muyambi, as a comforter, a mother, a heroine, and a soldier in God's army. She said that in 1989 on 6 February, she was received by Mrs Neddie Muyambi in her house. It was Sister Itayi's first time meeting her. Up to her last days on earth, Sister Itayi worked with Irene. Sister Itayi said that Irene was a fair lady with no discrimination who taught the nuns how to live an upright life in front of God and everyone. Sister Itayi said that Neddie was an advisor and a very humble woman who attended many, if not all, funerals she learnt of, of people known or unknown to her. She would lose sleep over comforting the bereaved. One good thing about her was that she was a forgiving woman. Even after one had wronged her, she kept her silence and peace amidst the provocation. Neddie was an encourager; she would tell people to hold fast to their faith, and she encouraged nuns not to breach their vows with God. Neddie was also a team player. For instance, when the St Agnes Children's Home was being painted, she took part, wielding a brush and painting the building. She led by example.

Neddie was a developer. She put her money, together with her husband, towards building the Trinity Zimbabwe Healing Chapel and all other related projects for the service of the needy and the sick.

In founding the religious Community of the Gifts of the Holy Fire (CZM), she played a very significant role. She prevailed where a lot of mothers failed. It is not easy to feed children who are not yours and who have no income. Most women think girls will take control of their marriages in the sense that they will disallow their husbands to work with females. Neddie allowed the safekeeping of orphans and young females. She allowed her and Lazarus's vision to succeed. She did not allow jealousy to get in the way of the propagation of God's Word. Up until her death, she never faltered. Neddie was a mother to all, a heroine for all, a saint. In 1995 at the Zimbabwe Healing Centre there, a Nyati family came to the mission haunted by evil spirits called Tamuzz (poltergeists). Neddie took her own clothes and gave them to this family who had been left naked by the ordeal. She supplied them with food from her own family reserves (Jongwe 2017).

Neddie was a CZM comforter. She loved all the nuns irrespective of where they came from, what their background or language was, and no matter their character or emotions. If they told her their problems, she presented herself as a true mother with motherly love. Neddie had a good listening ear and was very empathetic in nature. People felt relieved after talking to her. When the nuns came home from their different branches, she would pack food—rice, fruits, nuts—for them to take back with them to their respective CZM branches. When she visited their branches, she brought them goodies. She knew the nuns as her own children and treated them as such.

Sister Itayi said that the last time she spoke to Irene was on 19 November 2016, soon before Irene's death. Irene encouraged Sister Itayi to build a convent in Bulawayo. She also informed Sister Itayi that when she and her husband had built their projects at Gokwe, it was not an easy endeavour. Some people liked the idea and others disliked it, but, Irene said, one must not listen to negative comments and get discouraged. A community needs to grow and stand up for itself. She informed Sister Itayi that building the clinic had not been easy, but eventually she and her husband had managed to do it. Irene also encouraged Sister Itayi to keep receipts of the building material purchases. Irene said that the people who see the job being done will be the witnesses. She added, "Serve God, be united, and be one family. The CZM founder should see your convent before he dies. He must see you implement what he taught you. God will be happy. Worship God."

According to Sister Itayi, Irene Neddie loved to see God's work prosper, and she loved to please God and to serve God. She was a lover of all people, regardless of their differences. For instance, a lady with mental illness at Gokwe Centre grieved Irene's death. Anytime she saw one of the nuns, she would approached to express her condolences for the loss of a dear mother. Neddie was known by all from all walks of life. People of different denominations attended Neddie's funeral, as did politicians and non-Christians. The ministries of health, land development, and education were represented, including individuals from the President's Office. They all came to say goodbye to Neddie and bid her farewell. This showed that her great deeds since 1972 were appreciated in Gokwe and beyond.

Sister Itayi expressed concern, wondering why the Diocese of Central Zimbabwe had not honoured Irene as a saint. In politics, people are looked at for what they have done when they are made them heroes. What about in the church? The worldwide Church of England also looks at the good things one has done and gives them the honour they deserve. Sister Itayi said that when she visited the Anglican diocese of Njobe in Tanzania, she saw tombs in the cathedral. She learnt that founders of great projects are honoured in this world. These graves she saw are along the passage and by the choir place.

The Church of Christ is an Anglican cathedral in Stone Town, Zanzibar, Tanzania. It belongs to the Anglican Church of Tanzania. It is a historical landmark church, as well as one of the most prominent examples of early Christian architecture in East Africa. It was built in ten years, starting from 1873, based on a vision of Edward Steere, third Anglican bishop of Zanzibar, who actively contributed to the design. Edward Steere died of a heart attack when the cathedral was almost completed, and he was buried behind the altar ("Christ Church,_Zanzibar" 2017).

Sister Itayi went on to say that in the Diocese of Matabeleland in Zimbabwe, at St James Parish Church in Nyamandhlovu where she lives, the founder, Reverend Francis Boughtright, and his wife, Monica, were buried inside the St James main church building at Lady Chapel, under the altar. This means that the practice is nothing new in the Anglican Catholic system. In Matabeleland, some fathers of the Paul's Roman Catholic Church were buried in church buildings.

The Harare Anglican Diocese has tombs of soldiers who were buried there in memory of their good works. The Vatican Roman Catholic headquarters was built on top of Peter the disciple's grave. Peter, you are the rock. Why does it seem a shocking thing to bury our own Zimbabwean soldier in the army of God, a cofounder of great projects, inside a church building? What has shocked the nation? Apart from being an active Mothers' Union member for fifty-seven years, Neddie also performed great works which follow after her. They speak for her.

In the eighteenth century, some cathedrals and parish churches in cities were subject to intense pressure from burials such that the floors were in a state of upheaval (Fawcett 2001, p. 45).

There are a lot of famous people who were buried in the Winchester Cathedral in the United Kingdom. This goes to show that the practice of church burial should not cause any alarm. A person's deeds speak for themselves.

To bury someone under a roof is not new, not even in African custom.

In Botswana culture, a person can be buried in a house. Ecclesiastics 9:4–6 points out that the dead will not take anything from this earth. Where does our fear come from? Irene Neddie's spirit went to the Father, and all that's left is her body. We do not believe in the dead having anything to do with us. They can only pray.

Irene Neddie's works will be remembered. She has been buried in a cool holy place. She deserves the best. In Acts 9:36–39, Tabitha Dorcas is described as being remembered by the people she served. That reflects our position.

Rest in peace, hero in Christ.

Enlighten the Darkness: Research into Church and Chapel Burials

By Anesu Muyambi

For much of history, the church or churchyard was the only place for burials, until local councils and governments took over the responsibly because space was running out in church and churchyards. The great and the good could be interred inside the church. All other members of society were buried in the churchyard (Heritage Inspired 2016).

It is important that graves in the churchyard should face east, as the Lord will approach from the east at the final Day of Judgement. In the year 1971, we find, Bishop Swithin's body was transferred from the open air to the inside of Winchester Cathedral, and from that point we find his bones venerated, subdivided, and glorified inside the environment of the church building. It is unsurprising that Christians came to accept the dead and their remains in such an environment, in such proximity to the living in worship and prayer (Godricson 2015).

Bishops and martyrs began to be buried in the churches a long time ago. The cult of bones became not only prevalent but also acceptable, and in a strange manner the adherents of Christ became associated with what may be described as a "death cult" whereby a faith once based in hope, light, and resurrection became a faith associated with darkness and death. It seems that many people wanted to be buried in close proximity to the holy and royal monuments to honour the famous and the ignoble dead. Such practice became evident around the UK. Today cathedrals and chapels across the world contain both holy and royal people buried, as well as noble people and their family members, all in search of immortality.

Chancel floors around some English churches show signs of floor slabs having been pried up to bury people. It was also customary for the priest of the parish to be buried in the chancel, along with the lord of the manor. Most of the gentry would have been buried in the church, some with chapels and vaults for their memorials. Many of those memorials exist today. St David's Cathedral and or chapel is full of them. Some of these are very old. Most of our older local churches have their share of such memorials.

In 1664 if your family wanted to bury you (after your death) in the chancel of the church, which would involve lifting tiles and relaying them after the service, then there would be a fee. (The chancel is an area of the church near the altar for the use of clergy and choir. It is often separated from the nave by a screen or steps.

Many of the kings of England, their wives, and other relatives have been buried in Westminster Abbey. From the time of Edward the Confessor until the death of George II, in 1760, most kings and queens of England were buried there, except, notably, Edward IV, Henry VIII, and Charles I, who are buried in St George's Chapel in Windsor Castle. All monarchs who died after George II are buried in Windsor. Most were laid to rest in St George's Chapel.

Since the Middle Ages, aristocrats were buried inside chapels, while monks and other people associated with Westminster Abbey were buried in the Cloisters and other areas. One of these others was Geoffrey Chaucer, who was buried here, as he had apartments in the Abbey, where he was employed as master of the King's Works. Poets, writers, and musicians were buried or memorialised around Chaucer in what became known as Poets' Corner. Abbey musicians such as Henry Purcell were also buried in their place of work, which is a choir stall.

Another memorial in Westminster Abbey is the tomb of the Unknown Warrior, which is in the floor just inside the great west door, in the centre of the nave. This is the tomb of an unidentified British soldier killed on a European battlefield during the First World War. He was buried in the Abbey on 11 November 1920. There are many graves in the floors of the Abbey that you walk over, but this is the only grave on which it is forbidden to walk ("The Tomb of the Unknown Warrior" 2016).

Some notable people who have been buried in a church are William Shakespeare, Charles Dickens, and Isaac Newton.

(Holy Trinity Church, also known as Shakespeare's Church, in Stratford-upon-Avon, features a place known as Shakespeare's Grave, the site of the graves of William and Anne Shakespeare. This is the Holy Trinity Church in Stratford-upon-Avon. It is the site where William Shakespeare and close members of his family are buried inside.)

The title of lord or lady of the manor, or sometimes lord or lady of a property, indicated a person who owned property or land. The manor was the nucleus of English rural life. It was an administrative unit of an extensive area of land. The whole of it was owned originally by an individual called the lord of the manor. He lived in the big house called *the manor house.* Attached to it were many acres of grassland and woodlands called *the park.* These were lands designated for the personal use of the lord of the manor. Dotted all round were the enclosed homes and land occupied by the tenants of the manor. Many owners of these manors are buried in cathedrals or churches around England (Stephens 1983).

In the African culture, since time immemorial, senior members of the community were sometimes buried inside a hut which was used for preparing meals, right in front, where everyone could see the place. The name used to describe such a place was *chikuva*, which means "altar". *Chikuva* and *huva* are derived from *guva*, which means "the burial place of the ancestors". In Shona culture when a person dies, his or her body lies in state at the chikuva or huva. The father will act as a "priest" and the mother a "priestess", to borrow the terms from church religion. Members of the family and their friends and relatives are the "congregation". The hut is the "church". The chikuva is the "altar". Although the occasion looks like worship in the eyes of other religions, it is purely a family and communal affair between the Shona and their ancestors. There is no need for hired priests from outside. Although the hut looks like a church at such occasions, it is still a hut where people live, and everything that happens there is spiritual, social, economic, and sacred, including cooking and eating, in which the ancestors also partake (Chivaura 2015a).

Dead bodies pose no risk of infection unless the final illness was one of a very few which continue to pose a risk to the living for some time after death, in which case you will be told by medical personnel. Micro-organisms involved in the decomposition of a dead body are not pathogenic and cannot cause any kind of disease.

"My people are destroyed from lack of knowledge," says Hosea 4:6. We still are. As Africans, we choose and pick certain cultural practices that suit us, like a white wedding, and discard those that we dislike. Zimbabwe has closed one of its main cemeteries in Harare and there has been a call for cremation, again not in our culture. Shall we just stand and do nothing about it?

It's important that people understand the Christian and Anglican tradition. Although bishops run their dioceses independently, those dioceses still have their roots in the Church of England, and Church of the Province of Central Africa (CPCA) practices are still based primarily on the Church of England tradition. Each bishop is truly to act as a shepherd for his diocese. With the assistance of priests and deacons, bishops exercise their pastoral office over the portion of the people of God assigned to them, regardless of age, condition, or nationality, or whether permanently or temporarily residing in the diocese. Care must also be extended to those who have special needs, for example the home-bound, the disabled, and those who have fallen away from the church. The bishop must also foster good ecumenical relations, acting with kindness and charity towards those who are not in full communion with the church (Code of Canon Law 383).

If people mix church and spiritual mediums, they will have a problem with this act of burying people in chapels or churches. St Mary's Anglican Cathedral in Harare has graves placed in the cloisters and other places which invoke the memory of good things the departed contributed to Africa, the church and country alike. There are known graves of holders of the Victoria Cross. One of them is in Zimbabwe, honour a soldier who was cremated in Cape Town, South Africa and whose ashes were interred in Harare Anglican Cathedral. The Diocese of Central Zimbabwe is a member of the CPCA, which is part of the worldwide Anglican community with over seventy million members.

If you stand by God and God alone, it's spiritually fulfilling. When the Son of Man comes, what a great honour it will be to rise in glory from a place of worship. Not many will have this privilege.

Neddie was a philanthropist; she had a love for humanity and a sense of caring, and she nourished and developed people, enhancing what it meant to be human. She was a cofounder of Gokwe Children's Home, the Community of the Gifts of the Holy Fire, a spiritual healing centre, a clinic, a nursery school, a primary school, and a girls' secondary school.

Irene Neddie Muyambi was buried on private property, on private land, in a private chapel, which was the best honour she could have possibly been given by Reverend Canon Lazarus Muyambi, family and local people who appreciated her contribution to the Gokwe Community. This appreciation was shown by the number of people who attended her funeral to pay their last respects on the day. Present at the funeral were the church hierarchy and local authority leaders. It rained for twenty-four hours, from the time she arrived home to the time she was buried, which traditionally is a good sign for someone who did good. Neddie was a person who sought to promote the welfare of others, especially by being generous and giving donations of food, clothing, and money to good causes. She would spend hours and hours visiting the widowed, the sick, and the deprived and talking to people who needed spiritual, moral, and mental support.

The St Agnes Parish Church Is Closed and Locked after Neddie's Burial

On Sunday, 25 December 2016, St Agnes Church parishioners at Gokwe Centre came to church as usual. A Mass service was celebrated from 7 a.m. to 8 a.m. After Mass, the celebrant, who is the priest in charge, Reverend Elijah Mazula, addressed the congregation, discussing two circulars coming from Bishop Ishmael Mukuwanda. Reverend Mazula informed everyone that he had been away marking ZIMSEC papers in Harare. Upon coming back, he had found the two circulars waiting for his attention.

Reverend Mazula informed the congregation that Reverend John Makiwa had been stopped from serving as a priest in the Diocese of Central Zimbabwe. He said that Reverend Makiwa had also received a copy from the bishop with the reasons for this explained. The congregation was not told the reason why this had happened. However, Reverend Mazula advised the parishioners not to approach Reverend Makiwa anymore about illnesses, baptisms, bereavements, and so on, because he wouldn't be able to offer those services for the time being.

The St Agnes Parish Church Building locked

Reverend Makiwa celebrated Mass for about three hundred secondary schoolchildren, one thousand primary schoolchildren, and nuns of the Convent of the Community of the Gifts of the Holy Fire. He was an assistant to Reverend Lazarus in the healing ministry as he helped the eighty-three-year-old retired priest in the Diocese of Central Zimbabwe. Reverend Makiwa visited the St Agnes Parish church outstations. It is said that members of the Gwehava outstation were heartbroken. This meant no priest for them. Were the effects of this move taken into consideration? Reverend Mazula mentioned that because of clergy shortage and the fact that another priest had been stopped from practising as a priest in the Zhombe area, it was clear that no one would serve these outstations which John had served for no remuneration. John loves God and has served God all his life. He lived at Gokwe for the greater part of his life serving God.

Reverend Mazula then spoke about that Sunday, 25 December 2016, as the last service at St Agnes Parish, citing that the bishop had said he would not visit the parish henceforth. Reverend Mazula said he had been instructed to find an alternative place for worship. He said he is under the bishop and follows his instruction. Therefore, per the bishop's order, the church would be locked to safeguard the property of the church.

This was on Christmas Day, a day when Christians celebrate the birth of Christ and his coming into the world to serve humanity.

It is believed that a church building is a public place that should serve the community. Even if there is no Sunday service, people need time to walk into the church and meditate. The church is a place to sit quietly and have quality time with the Creator.

Reverend Lazarus had built this church in 1973 with the help of a few church members. He, the builder, and his family moulded the bricks. He went to ZISCO in Kwekwe to ask for roofing material because the diocese had asked him to cut poles from the bush for use in roofing the church building. See the narrative written by Neddie in 1974 about the building of this church in Part I of this book, the chapter entitled Neddie Writes about the Building of St Agnes Area.

Below is a list of the clergy who worked at St Agnes Gokwe Primary School, in their respective chronological order:
- Reverend Gwetu
- Reverend Mswelando
- Catechist Sitotombe
- Reverend Mtero
- Reverend Malety
- Subdeacon Kupfuwa
- Reverend Fengu
- Reverend Masabalala
- Reverend Muyambi, first priest in charge at St Agnes Anglican Church Parish, Gokwe, 1972
- Reverend Friar Vanny (CZM)
- Reverend Friar Makweya (CZM)
- Reverend Sherewa
- Reverend Chapata
- Reverend Kangwende
- Reverend Mazula
- Reverend Makamure

It was from 1972 that progress began to be noticed, progress that continues until today. Muyambi village caters for all denominations as people created by God. People from all walks of life are welcome. From day one, when the diocese could not financially help the Muyambis, the latter spent their money and sourced donations; well-wishers helped them; and their own children living abroad provided funds to help their parents' projects.

Amidst all the aforementioned events, Lazarus dreamt of seeing a big lion and an axe, the latter provided on a string from heaven. He attacked the lion, destroying its head by landing a blow on its the forehead. This was a dream of victory. His children went on a ten-day fast from 9 January 2017 to 19 January 2017 to pray for their father's health and their father's projects.

As mentioned above, when Reverend Mazula informed the congregation about the two circulars from the bishop, he asked the congregation to air their views about the issue. If anyone was not happy about the decision, he instructed them to move to an alternative place and to continue coming to St Agnes Parish Church. Since there was no response, he asked members to feel free to talk to him afterwards.

Father Mazula went on to inform the congregation that, according to the long-term plan, a letter had been sent to Gokwe Town Council on 28 November 2016 to request a larger portion of land upon which to build a church, because the current plot was small and crowded—not big enough, he said. He said the short-term plan was to seek an alternative place of worship. Reverend Mazula said the diocese was going to help them to build the new church once they were given the new land. He indicated that they might return to St Agnes Parish once the dust has settled. He also reiterated that the church would remain the property of the Diocese of Central Zimbabwe until further notice.

Reverend Mazula went on to mention that Izwi Muyambi had approached him the previous day after evensong and courteously informed him that he had not managed to contact him when he was away in Harare to inform him about the putting up of a wire fence to demarcate the St Agnes Parish from all the independent projects at Gokwe of which Reverend Lazarus is the founder and owner. Izwi had cited security of students as one major reason for the fencing. Reverend Mazula assured the congregation that this fence had the bishop's blessings and that the project was already in the pipeline. He also said that a small gate had been put up so that church members would be able to access the toilets, as there are no public toilets at the parish. Father Mazula said there was no fighting but that the whole issue was being peacefully resolved

Reverend Canon L. T. Muyambi, addressing mourners at his wife's funeral, emphasised the need for Gokwe to have a diocese. He showed great concern about priests who are deployed to the parish and then sit and do nothing. He said they just sit in offices and make no progress. He cried that Gokwe needed a diocese, and it needed priests who went right into Gokwe like he used to do years ago. He applauded the Roman Catholic Church for taking giant steps towards development. Gokwe is a very big district that needs to stand on its own, he said.

The Community of the Gifts of the Holy Fire Retreat

**Reverend Lazarus Muyambi (Right)
with Friars and Nuns**

The nuns of the religious Community of the Gifts of the Holy Fire (CZM) meet once a year for their three-day retreat. This takes place after Christmas at the CZM arch-house at Gokwe. The two CZM branches, St James's Nyamandhlovu and St Patrick's Gweru come to Gokwe. It used to be that they all came without fail, but for the first time since the commencement of the religious community in 1978, the St Patrick's branch turned down an invitation to the retreat on 27 December 2016 extended to them by the arch-sister Theresa (CZM). The reason they cited was that they were busy at work, which is not always the case—and it is against the religious community rule of life to be too busy for the retreat. In any event, the retreat progressed without them. It was later stated that they had held their own retreat. This was the first time in history for the CZM to hold two separate retreats, instead of coming together as usual. Whoever had facilitated the second retreat was not authorised to do so by the founder and owner of the community. What did this refusal to attend mean? Was the CZM still one community? If the St Patrick's branch were to opt out, then they might have to change their rule of life, name, and uniform, because the CZM was born in Gokwe.

On the night Neddie's body lay in state before burial, it is said that senior nuns of the CZM had not attended the all-night vigil to pay their last respects to Neddie, the woman who had been their mother at some point in their lives when they were vulnerable girls. One of the speakers that night queried where senior sisters of the CZM were, as he had seen only junior sisters. Those who had benefitted from Neddie's endless love in her home for years kept away that night. Most of them were from St Patrick's branch. That alone, never mind their failure to attend the 2016 retreat for the first time, was a clear statement.

What Caused the Division in the CZM?

I talked to a few nuns about what could have caused the community to become divided, as some members went off into the world to start a new life and some left for the St James's branch and others for the St Patrick's branch. Despite the efforts of Lazarus and Neddie to look after them, educate them, and send some of them abroad, they still abandoned the rule of life, their founder, and the supporting community.

Below are some of the reasons for what caused the division I learnt from dialogues I had with some community members.

It was stated that the arch-sister at a certain period:

- Bullied nuns and friars. For instance, one sister had a new jacket bought for her by her mum, but the arch-sister took it from her and gave it to her own niece at home. This was very hurtful to this nun.
- Practised unfairness and injustice in handling senior and junior nuns and friars.

- Gave herself and other senior nuns advantage over the junior nuns.
- Did not listen to junior nuns' opinions, but looked down upon them.
- Verbally abused some nuns and friars, humiliated them, and reduced them to nothing in public.
- Fought hard to cause animosity between Reverend Lazarus and his children, making herself family. This did not please some members of the family and community.
- Never appreciated the efforts of colleagues. For her, it was "Just do as I say". Most sisters and friars, with tears in their eyes, escaped this unfair treatment by going out into the world.
- Allowed unfairness to prevail in the education sector. She picked and chose the nuns or friars she liked, to send them to school, to college, or out of the country.
- Was power hungry, as were others in the community.
- Was, along with other senior nuns, a bad influence, encouraging junior sisters to leave Gokwe for other branches. For instance, one nun at Gokwe was visited in her room by a senior nun from abroad. The former was asked to leave Reverend Canon Lazarus Muyambi and join the other branch. This young nun got very cross, challenged the visiting nuns, and dismissed them. They had to apologise. She said she asked them why the founder of such a good community should be abandoned after all these years. "Now that he is an old man, do we have to leave him?" She informed them that the devil was working towards disaster and destruction through them. She assured them that, come hail, come thunder, she would support the founder and owner of the CZM religious community until death.
- Encouraged love of money, which caused disunity. For instance, a senior nun would be seen giving money or clothes to her family when they visited, yet there was hunger and poverty within the community. This act did not sit well with other nuns.
- Unequally distributed resources. Some nuns lacked feminine needs, for example.

Other reasons cited for the division are the following:

- Some working-class nuns were supposed to put their money into the community coffers, but some of them were selfish and did not do so. This caused the unemployed nuns to suffer, as they lacked basic needs. The founders, Lazarus and Neddie, continued to support the community from their coffers whenever there was a need. They continued to create jobs for the nuns so they could earn a living, for example at the schools and a clinic.
- The founders' family and other well-wishers would send consignments of goods from the United Kingdom for CZM and the orphanage, but certain items were unfairly distributed.
- There was a lot of gossip, some senior nuns reporting the juniors to the founder to get them into trouble. This caused a lot of commotion.
- The founders, Lazarus and Neddie, lost lots of money by having sent some nuns and friars abroad, hoping to develop the community economically, and then seeing them leave the CZM, opting to support these other branches and their own families.
- At one time, the mother of one of the senior nuns was ill. This nun sent a junior nun to her rural home to look after her mum as her carer, which is not part of the community rules. The mother later came to the Healing Centre and was cared for by other nuns, while her own daughter pretended to be busy. This hurt the mother. She complained to other nuns, asking why her own daughter was not taking care of her.
- There were a lot of lies being told within the community.

Those who remained were fighters. They have remained strong.

One senior nun had come to Gokwe from the United Kingdom. After a week, she informed the founder that she was going to another branch to bid them farewell, after which she would return to Gokwe. Surprisingly, she never came back, which was a sign of disrespect to Lazarus and Neddie, who had given her a life in Gokwe. Lazarus has openly informed the nuns that they may go if they wish, but he has asked them not to lie and say that they are coming back when they know very well they are going for good. Just be honest and say goodbye.

One of the nuns is believed to be at war with the founder of the CZM. She seems not to have proper facts about how the CZM was started. It is untrue when she says she is the founder of the community. Following is a discussion of how the CZM was started. This woman has an apparent lack of appreciation for the man and woman who looked after the first nuns in their house including her, providing them with basic needs, whilst at the same time battling with the Diocese of Matabeleland to start a community of nuns and friars. (See Bishop Robert Mercer's letter, available upon request.)

Who Is the Founder of CZM Religious Community, and How Did It Begin?

As mentioned before, the channel of God in the healing ministry Lazarus Canon Muyambi arrived in Gokwe in 1972. Most of the people he healed were girls. The girls who were healed were many. Over eighty-two were exorcised of evil spirits. Most of these had been possessed by witchcraft demons. After receiving healing, some of them wanted to stay at the parish.

Following are the words of Reverend Canon Muyambi:

I then decided to travel with them in the district, doing God's work. They would give testimonies of how God had healed them. These testimonies were so touching and encouraging to those who listened to them. They witnessed for Christ the healer. These girls were good singers as well, so they would sing in spirit as I prayed for the sick. Through them the Anglican church became very popular in the Gokwe district and beyond. This attracted many more girls to join them. I was very invested in theology on girls' issues. I had a very strong St Agnes Guild of girls who were virgins. My emphasis was on virginity. My wife, Neddie, prepared them for marriage. I emphasised the cultural practice of going into marriage with an egg placed on cornmeal in a small basket. The girl's aunt would approve of this publicly in the church. The parents loved this practice, which is of an old culture and is very godly, and encourages girls to keep their virginity for their future husband. Jesus himself was born of the Virgin Mary. I did talk a lot about how St Agnes the Martyr was killed in Rome because of her virginity.

So, St Agnes Guild grew bigger and stronger, attracting girls even from other churches and denominations. Many people began speaking poorly about my association with girls. The Lord said to me, "Hear what people are saying, fill your car with petrol, and take these girls around the community. Do not worry about what people say." The girls loved me and I loved them. These girls, my family, and other members of the congregation helped to mould bricks for the St Agnes Parish church building. Boys joined as well. I built up a strong church choir which used to sing in church and in music competitions. This attracted many people to come and join the Anglican Church. A lady called Bridget Malisa used to visit us and educate girls on different things about growing up.

When the church building was complete, it was officially opened by Bishop Mark Wood. In 1977 Bishop Mark Wood brought me pictures of nuns and influenced me to educate girls to become nuns. I preached madly about becoming nuns. After casting out evil spirits from most of the girls, I started asking those who wanted to serve God as nuns to come see me. Initially four girls came forward. Sister Eugenia Munyoro, who was doing grade 7 at St Agnes Primary School and residing in my house, decided to become a nun. After grade 7, she went to St Patrick's Secondary School to do first form. I informed the bishop that Eugenia wanted to be a nun. She was sent to St Augustine Mission in Mutare. Eugenia had previously had some contact with nuns at Kana Mission in Gokwe. During my school days, I had attended school with some nuns at St Paul's Musami. This influenced me to accept the bishop's suggestion. I came to love the idea, and I started a religious community at Gokwe. I had also been in contact with white nuns who were teachers at St Paul's Musami. I just loved the whole idea.

The other three who became nuns were Gladys Chimhou, Esnati Chikuse, and Mable Hamandishe. I informed Matenga ("the heavens") that I had girls willing to be nuns. "Can you help me to start a community?" I was advised to inform the bishop, who was now Robert Mercer, that I wanted to start a religious community. The bishop discouraged me and asked me to give up on the idea, saying I did not have a degree and had no food to give the girls. He also said I was all right with my family and that starting a community entailed clothing and feeding them, which was not easy. I argued with him in writing, saying that I would find food for them and would mould bricks to build shelter for them. At this time, the girls were living in my house, sharing food and bedding with my family. My wife was a teacher, so we had enough money to survive. They helped me with all the duties at the Centre.

As I have mentioned, given that Bishop Robert Mercer discouraged me from starting a community of nuns, I continued to battle and argue with him, telling him that I was being advised by the Spirit of the Lord to start a religious community. He warned and informed me that the church was poor and was not going to support me. He called a meeting in Bulawayo, where he was based. At that time, we fell under the Diocese of Matabeleland. I went to attend the meeting with Mable Hamandishe, who had a gift of prophesy and was living in my house.

Present at the meeting were:
- Bishop Robert Mercer
- Reverend Lazarus Muyambi
- Sister Truder (PhD) of the Anglican Community of Nuns
- Sister Marilyn of the Anglican Community of Sisters
- Reverend Masuku of St Columba Parish Church
- Mable Hamandishe from my parish (she was my spiritual advisor, as she had a gift of prophetic utterances)

Mable and I were accommodated in the upper rooms. We were informed that Sister Truder was in hospital. I went to pray for her, and she was instantly healed, immediately gaining the strength to come to St Andrew's House, where we were based.

The Meeting

The meeting was scheduled for the following day. I was in spirit and Mable was in spirit. One could feel the presence of the Holy Spirit all around us. I was asked to start talking about why I wanted to start a religious community of nuns and friars. I explained that I needed helpers at the Zimbabwe Healing Centre. I also needed help with singing in the choir as I moved around to the twenty congregations I had started around Gokwe district. Singing attracted many people to join the church.

However, Gokwe was full of witches, wizards, witch doctors, and non-Christians drumming everywhere at night. We used to sing "Guide Me, O Thou Great Redeemer". People liked our way of singing, which was very powerful. Gokwe is very remote and is the largest district in Zimbabwe. Gokwe South and North had come under my control. It was hard work, so I needed helpers in God's field. I travelled all around, casting out evil spirits, accompanied by holy angels.

After I had explained my rule of life and why I wanted to start this community, the bishop asked if anyone present had a complaint or objection. Everyone agreed that it was a noble idea. Sister Truder, mother of the white religious community, agreed too. It was unanimously agreed that my idea was bright and great. While we were still in the meeting, Sister Mable gave me a bit of prophetic advice indicating that I should not ask questions anymore. Therefore, I kept quiet.

We went to Gokwe. Sister Esnati, Sister Gladys, and another girl were postulants at that time. They were sent to associate with nuns at St Augustine Penalonga in Mutare. They studied about their vocation for three months. Postulant Esnati gave up and returned to Gokwe, where she continued with her postulant stage. She said she had not liked the treatment she'd gotten from those at St Augustine. Sister Gladys continued, finished her three months, and returned to Gokwe.

I wrote the bishop to say I had completed building the convent for nuns and that it needed to be officially opened. Bishop Robert Mercer said he could not oblige me unless there was a chapel. I had to move all the girls from one dormitory and change it into a chapel. One of the parishioners, Edwin Munyoro, worked with me by going into the forest to cut poles for the roofing. I got corrugated iron sheets from St Luke's Parish Church in Kwekwe, which is a white community church. They were happy to help, and they serviced my car as well. I returned to Gokwe and roofed the chapel. I invited the bishop to come in that year, 1977.

The Opening of the Convent of the Community of the Gifts of the Holy Fire

The bishop came with nine nuns from Bulawayo. Three were postulants and six were novices. They wore *makwati* (wooden) shoes. The three postulants I had been accommodating in my house moved into the new convent, which was now going to be their permanent dwelling place. We were an independent organisation. We served ourselves, the church, and the people. The Holy Spirit was active. Angels were active. Our girls were active. Many wanted to join us.

When I realised that the first convent was full, I asked the holy angels for advice. The Lord said, "Lazarus, do you think they will give you a bigger piece of land?" I went to Gokwe District Council and asked for a place to build a bigger convent. My request was granted and the land was shown to me. Mr Chinho, the Gokwe town council surveyor came and measured three and half hectares for us. I straight away began to mould bricks with sisters, well-wishers, and my family. We moulded many bricks. I looked for a planner to create a plan for us. I found one in Gweru; his name was Bishop.

Once I found a builder, the construction started. I paid the workers for the job myself, as there was no money provided from any other source. The floor was completed at twelve midnight. Our determination was high. It is a beautiful convent. Large enough to accommodate fifty nuns, it still stands today. I asked Minister Victoria Chitepo to come and officially open the convent. She came, and in her speech she highly praised the idea of starting a religious community in Gokwe.

At the present day, we have three groups of nuns. One is at St Patrick's Chiwundura; another at St James's Nyamandhlovu; and the other here at Gokwe. We have two sisters working abroad as nurses; unfortunately, they no longer support us here, so we continue to struggle to make ends meet. Our providing support for them to go abroad was aimed at developing ourselves at Gokwe, but it ended up not benefitting us at all, so we continue to ask for God's involvement in our plight.

How Did the Monastery Begin?

Friar Vanny being inducted into the community of CZM

Vanny Masukume's arrival was the beginning of the monastery of friars. He joined after running away from his family, having come to be a friar. His father followed with a big knobkerrie, threatening to kill me. He told his son to pack his clothes and return home. I was very polite and asked the man to take his son back home. Surprisingly Vanny left all his clothes, and carried an empty suitcase. Once he was home, he left his suitcase in the house and pretended to be going to the garden. He disappeared and ran back to St Agnes Parish. When the father checked Vanny's suitcase, it was empty. Suddenly it dawned on him that Vanny had returned to me. I suppose he got very furious, but he gave up and left Vanny to do what pleased his heart, to serve God as a friar. Vanny, as mentioned, was the first friar to join the monastery.

Many more came and went. Friar Vanny trained as a builder and later as a priest. He eventually left the community as well. The friars are now on their own. They are no longer with the nuns. I as the founder of the community separated them so they could do their own thing and establish themselves. As already mentioned, several of them left the community for various reasons, some because of moral weakness, and others for jobs because they had obtained professional education. At the diocesan synod in 1997, I stated to the delegates that I had stopped accepting and inducting friars into the community.

Any new friars were encouraged to join Friar Joshua Musiyambiri. I found that keeping them together was morally unproductive. This is not a strange idea, because in some Anglican religious communities all boys eventually leave for marriage.

This is the journey I have travelled to develop the Community of the Gifts of the Holy Fire. I am the founder and owner of the community, which was approved by the Diocese of Matabeleland in 1977 and 1978, before Zimbabwe attained its independence from the colonial regime in 1980. I am very sorry for its dissolution. I have worked very hard to provide food, water, clothes, education, and transport for the nuns, compromising my own family to care for their needs.

—Reverend Canon Lazarus Muyambi

Mrs J. N. Muyambi's Favourite Prayer in Remembrance of Christ's Works at the Zimbabwe Healing and Manger Centre

Teach us, good Lord, to serve thee as thou deserves,
To give and not to count the cost,
To toil and not to seek for rest,
To labour and not to ask for reward,
To fight and not heal the wounds,
To praise and not to seek for praise,
Save that knowing we do thy will through Jesus Christ our Lord.
Amen.

—St Ignatius Loyola

Irene Neddie Muyambi's Memorial Service, United Kingdom

ST GEORGES CHURCH
BIRMINGHAM

Memorial Service

Irene Neddie Muyambi

SAT 18TH MARCH 2017
TIME 11AM

Reverend Canon Edias Basvi speaks

Speaking at Irene's memorial service, Reverend Canon Edias Basvi said to those in attendance that they had gathered to testify and celebrate the life of the late Mrs Irene Neddie Muyambi and, in the process, to comfort her female and male children, her daughters-in-law, her sons-in-law, and all her grandchildren with whom we worship in Zimbabwe Anglicans in Birmingham (ZAB), Zimbabwe Anglicans fellowship - North West branch and Zimbabwe National Anglican Fellowship (ZINAFE).

Reverend Basvi started by looking at the name of Irene Neddie, saying that people can discern some hidden truths of a person's life by studying their name or names.

He said he looked up her name in a book of names and their meanings and came up with the following:

The name Irene comes from Greek language and means "peace". The name Neddie comes from Old English and means "rich", or "happy", or "guardian". From this, it is clear that names have a lot of bearing on people's lives.

Reverend Basvi said that a quiet person preserves his or her dignity. Mrs Muyambi had these two important virtues: quietness and an always smiling nature. He said quietness drives away difficulties, and that a smile decorates one's appearance with joy and dissolves all difficulties. The book of Proverbs confirms this, as it states, "Those who are sure of themselves do not talk all the time, people who stay calm have real insight. After all, even a fool may be thought to be wise and intelligent if he stays quiet and keeps his mouth shut" (Proverbs 17:27).

Reverend Basvi said that Mrs Muyambi always displayed a calm attitude. That was why he said that a quiet person preserves his or her own dignity, as one's dignity may only be praised or criticised after one speaks. He said that those in attendance had known Mrs Muyambi as a clergyman's wife who was calm and always dignified. She could align herself with people of both lower classes and higher classes. It only took an encounter with her at her workplace for one to know that she was educated. She was calm and always wearing a smile on her face; that was her language.

One would only hear Mrs Muyambi's voice when she was singing or praying in the company of other women. Musical talent was inherent in her family of origin, the Mashinyas. Reverend Basvi first knew her father, Mr Mashinya, from St Columbus Church in Bulawayo during the years 1965 to 1968. Her father used to sing in a beautiful baritone voice as an old man. Reverend Basvi used to sing in the church choir with Irene's brother Herbert Mashinya, together with the retired bishop Elijah Masuko, when he was a deacon at St Columbus. Because of his outstanding performance in both vocal and instrumental music, Herbert had been sent to Kwanongoma, a college specialising in music in Bulawayo, Zimbabwe.

Reverend Basvi went on to say that Mrs Muyambi was a champion in comforting the bereaved. She was an expert. When Reverend Basvi's youngest son died in the United Kingdom in the year 2009, the family waited for two weeks before the body arrived in Zimbabwe. Mrs Muyambi went to visit the Basvi family in the week the body was expected to arrive. She took the whole week to comfort and strengthen Mrs Basvi, until the deceased was laid to rest.

Reverend Basvi's daughter Shelter died in 2015 while the family were in the United Kingdom. They could not go home because of Mrs Basvi's illness. Mrs Irene Muyambi spent the whole week with Reverend Basvi's children, representing Mrs Basvi, who couldn't be present. Other clergy wives would go back to their homes in the evenings during the week, but Mrs Muyambi could not go back to Gokwe. She soldiered on until after Shelter's burial.

The same thing happened during the time of the unveiling of Shelter's tombstone. The girls who had travelled home from the United Kingdom for the unveiling found Mrs Muyambi at home with the children as if she were the lady of the Basvi household.

It is hard for anyone to match the deeds of this noble woman or her character. Those who knew Mrs Muyambi and who emulate her are able to point to her as the inspiration for their good works.

The message delivered at Irene's burial was very clear: if any of Mrs Muyambi's children behave in accordance with the Word of God like their Mother did, their service to the Lord will not be in vain.

Reverend Basvi went on to say that the good service of a person attracts is remembered for time immemorial after they are gone

He said he testified according to what good Mrs Muyambi had done for him and his family. He said that she served others just as well, adding that Mrs Muyambi would offer much more than just comfort in times of need, providing many other different services. Mrs Muyambi today is missed by many people for her calmness, peacefulness, and service.

In the midst of confusion and misunderstanding, she was a person who could only encourage calm and peace. "Blessed are the peace makers for they shall be called the children of God" (Matthew 5:9). Whenever the going got tough, she would sing a chorus common to her contemporaries: "Women of the Mothers' Union are present for the difficult times!"

Mrs Muyambi was good at receiving visitors in her home, as the Word of God says in Hebrews: "Remember to welcome strangers in your homes. There were some who did that, and welcomed angels without knowing it" (Hebrews 13:2).

Visiting Irene in her home, one would find that she expressed her heartfelt joy and provided all she could to entertain her guests. She would not let her visitors leave empty-handed. She was far too generous, far too good to be true. Mrs Muyambi always displayed an unwavering humility and piety at worship services.

During worship services in church, Mrs Muyambi had the good habit of kneeling without tiring. It did not matter how long the prayer would be, she would be on her knees when everyone else had taken their seats.

Be Confident and Determined

Reverend Basvi said that he wished to remind Irene's children that even though their mother was no more, they should be strong in faith and begin from where their mother had left off in doing good. If they were determined to please her and to meet her in the next life, they needed to just simply follow in her footsteps.

The Mashinya family, into which Irene was born, had played their part in commended her to Christian life as a girl child. She got married and brought up her family in the Christian way. Irene's faith was great, and by faith is the only way that leads to eternal life. With faith, one has the hope of being raised to life on the last day.

Reverend Basvi further said that people have no permanent dwelling here on earth. On that day, Neddie's children were witnessing and testifying of their mother, who knew that she had no permanent dwelling here on earth, and who therefore had laboured for her better, heavenly dwelling, where the mourners believe she has gone. People like Neddie are the people we confidently say God is not ashamed to have them call him their God, because they served him faithfully.

Irene's spirit testifies that she had given up her pride, was someone who was known to be humble, and was now content and at peace like a baby, quiet in its mother's arms. It is our hope that Mrs Muyambi's soul will rest in peace and be raised to eternal life.

Ruth Elphinston Speaks

Speaking at the memorial service of Irene, Ruth said, "In Genesis the Lord God said, 'It is not good for the man to be alone. I will make a helper suitable for him' (Genesis 2:18). This might mean a suitable helper who goes before you, who paves the way for you, who makes your journey easier."

Although Ruth and her daughter Sarah spent a short week as guests in the home of Irene and Lazarus, it was abundantly clear to them that she had been indeed a wonderful and suitable helper for Lazarus on his journey of faith in God.

During their few days in Gokwe, Ruth and Sarah had been treated to a full, comprehensive tour of all aspects of the mission. Ruth said it was clear to her that Irene had played a vital role in working with Lazarus, to establish the many aspects of St Agnes Mission life. Irene was just what God had in mind when he spoke of a helpmate.

Not long after Ruth and Sarah had arrived in Lazarus and Neddie's home, they had, over lunch, thankfully been excused from eating the traditional bowl of sadza and were kindly provided with cornflakes instead. Ruth and Sarah were very surprised to hear that Irene was heading into the nursery class of the mission's primary school. Interestingly, Ruth thought, *Maybe she is going to check that things are running smoothly*—a very Western approach for a seventy-year-old.

Irene was doing nothing of the sort. She was, in fact, heading off for a full day's teaching in the hot Zimbabwean sun. Age seemed to be irrelevant to Irene; there was a need, and she had the skills and servant heart required to fulfil that need.

At the time, Ruth suspected that this was how Irene had always lived her life. As the week progressed and Ruth and Sarah saw more of the work of the mission, their suspicions were confirmed.

Later that week, they were absolutely thrilled to be treated to a performance of the nursery class's nativity play.

Irene, complete with her beautiful wide-brimmed hat, presided over the whole event, which was held outside the nursery classroom in the bright hot sunshine

The enthusiastic singing and the loud, clear narration were both testament to the vision she and Lazarus had for education. Her calm, capable, and resourceful approach carried the whole production, with shepherds arriving costumed in a set of old brown gabardine-style raincoats and with the imaginative use of many props.

Irene and Lazarus's passion for children and education in particular pervaded the mission.

Ruth asked the audience how many women they knew who were happy to share their back garden with five hundred or so primary schoolchildren and over two hundred secondary schoolgirls, not to mention the family of St Agnes Children's Home?

The primary school is a wonderful example of the depth and breadth of the Muyambis' vision for the education of children.

Ruth and Sarah were stunned by the performance that the schoolchildren put on specially for them. They were mesmerised by the dumb-bells routine and highly impressed with the drama and singing, and they marvelled at the standard of everything the children did.

"This kind of thing doesn't happen overnight or without people of vision," Ruth said. It was clear to her that Irene and Lazarus had been faithful to their passion.

During Ruth and Sarah's week's stay, Lazarus took them to a small village where he had clearly set his heart on starting a bush school. Ruth remembered thinking, *This man is unstoppable. Irene must have the faith and patience of a saint!*

Ruth said she didn't know how that project was going but that it wouldn't surprise her in the least if the school was now up and running. But she was sure that with the help of Izwi and others, the foundations she saw in October 2010 would become a fully operational high school for girls, a school Ruth believed that at some point she would get to visit again!

Ruth went on to say that it was truly awe-inspiring to visit each part of the mission and reflect on the journey that Irene and Lazarus must have travelled together in order for their vision to become a reality, especially given—if she could be so bold as to say—the difference between English and African timekeeping! She felt she was breathing in a lifetime of challenging work and faith, and years of devotion, that had nurtured a vision from a seed to a mature plant.

Ruth said she would have loved to have spent a week with Lazarus and Irene during the early days of establishing the mission.

Irene was the mother of a healthy brood of natural children, but it seemed to Ruth that Irene held the place of mother in the hearts of the children and staff involved in every aspect of the mission, not least those involved in St Agnes Children's Home. Ruth and Sarah were overwhelmed by the love and care that went into the running of this home.

Ruth said she remembered the spotlessly clean bedrooms and a real sense of family and belonging. To sustain such a vision through the years of hardship and challenge that Zimbabwe has faced reflects, she said, something of the depth of the mother's heart Irene had.

It is one thing to share your garden with children, and quite another to share your kitchen with other women. But this is precisely what Irene seemed to do, and in an utterly calm manner!

It appeared to Ruth and Sarah that on most days of the week, Sister Phoebe and other members of the convent family enjoyed the love and care found in the Muyambi home, and much friendship and fellowship was enjoyed over mealtime.

The peanut butter and spinach recipe was delicious, but Ruth wasn't quite so sure about the chicken stew complete with chicken feet. One afternoon Irene took Ruth and Sarah to visit the various impressive vegetable gardens. Along with water pumps and other small business enterprises, the mission had a feel of a cottage industry which could sustain itself amidst the tough economic climate of the country.

Sadly, Ruth said, she had only spent a brief time in Irene's company, but it was long enough for her to believe that the following words of scripture express the kind of woman that she was.

The Wife of Noble Character

A wife of noble character who can find?
She is worth far more than rubies.
Her husband has full confidence in her
and lacks nothing of value.
She brings him good, not harm,

all the days of her life.
She selects wool and flax
and works with eager hands.
She is like the merchant ships,
bringing her food from afar.
She gets up while it is still night;
she provides food for her family
and portions for her female servants.
She considers a field and buys it;
Out of her earnings she plants a vineyard.
She sets about her work vigorously;
her arms are strong for her tasks.
She sees that her trading is profitable,
and her lamp does not go out at night.
In her hand she holds the distaff
and grasps the spindle with her fingers.
She opens her arms to the poor
and extends her hands to the needy.
When it snows, she has no fear for her household;
for all of them are clothed in scarlet.
She makes coverings for her bed;
she is clothed in fine linen and purple.
Her husband is respected at the city gate,
where he takes his seat among the elders of the land.
She makes linen garments and sells them,
and supplies the merchants with sashes.
She is clothed with strength and dignity;
she can laugh at the days to come.
She speaks with wisdom,
and faithful instruction is on her tongue.
She watches over the affairs of her household
and does not eat the bread of idleness.
Her children arise and call her blessed;
her husband also, and he praises her:
"Many women do noble things,
but you surpass them all."
Charm is deceptive, and beauty is fleeting;
but a woman who fears the Lord is to be praised.
Honor her for all that her hands have done,
and let her works bring her praise at the city gate.
(Proverbs 31)

Neddie's Family Speaks of Their Mother

Dorothea Matsveru

Sweet Mother in Heaven, When Will I See You Again?

My name is Chiwoniso Dorothea Matsveru. I am married to Jacob Matsveru. We are blessed with four children, namely Tatenda, Tinomukudza, Tariro, and Tinaye.

Born on 2 October 1961, I am the eldest child in the family. My mother, Irene Neddie Muyambi, was the firstborn child in her family, and my dad is also the firstborn in his family, making me the eldest grandchild in both families. My mother used to always say to me that she was proud of this fact, and she always encouraged me to take responsibility for all the grandchildren in both clans. The name Neddie means "guardian of wealth", and this is portrayed in what she left behind. Ours is a big loss, because she was last child to die in her family.

Mum was my grade 1 teacher. She gave me a good educational foundation. Where I am now in terms of education and progress clearly spells this out. She brought me up in a very special way. That's why I am given a leadership post in each job I get. I am a jack of all trades. I would say that at six years of age I was already a little mother. And it was the same with all my siblings, because Mum was a good trainer. At church, we all helped a lot as well. I could recite Mathew 5:1–12 by heart at that age. She never spoiled us at all, and we were taught to be handy and do things for ourselves, even though we had housemaids all the time. Maids and garden helpers were treated like family. Mum instilled love into our hearts from an early age; thus we love and help people, especially the needy. We go to funerals and visit the sick, because that is how we were bred.

Mum was a singer. She left us all the singing gift. We are called the Trinity Family Singers. We sing in church, at weddings, and at funerals. Mum always dressed smart; stockings, suit, hat, and a matching scarf was the order of the day. Our diet consisted of nutritious food, including fruits and vegetables.

Dad dictated the pace, and Mum supported whatever Dad taught. Sometimes we could not tell who was interested in what, as they sang from the same hymn sheet. They were both florists, but Dad is in favour of fruit trees. Mum was very much into gardening and the orchard.

Mum was a tailor, having made most of our clothes and hand-knitted cardigans for us, and was the best cook I have ever met. Our home was a visitors' home. She would bake cake and scones, always ensuring that family, church members, and those in need went away with full bellies. No visitors ever left empty-handed. She showed her kindness by giving some people clothes and blankets. Being charitable was very natural to her. She passed on this trait to us. We tend to give a lot. It is the norm for us as well. God gave us spouses who understand where we come from, and they are all part and parcel of the giving game. Mum did great works, comforting and caring for orphans, the sick, widows, and widowers. She accepted having nuns live under the same roof as she, something which most African women can't fathom. She was amazing. She told me people who did not like or love her. She told me names of people who offended her, but she gave them all true love, gifts, and support. For our mum, we must continue to love such people and do good to all humankind.

When we worked hard to get money and stuff to help with our parents' projects, Mum gave me a scripture to read, Luke 10:2: "But rejoice that your names are written in heaven." So, for whatever we may do or accomplish, we need to do it for God's glory.

Mum knew that she was going to die soon. When I went for my grandmother's funeral in February 2016, Mum said she was not ready to die as her mum had. She struggled to come to terms with her own death, and she eventually became ready. She also said she felt it was better for her to die before my dad did, as there were many issues and problems with their Gokwe projects that she felt she could not manage to solve, such as the title deeds, if Dad died first. When I went back in August, she asked me to ask her sister-in-law Susan Mashinya to go to Gokwe so that she could tell her personally that she could live freely in the house she is in B/F 28, as Mum was the remaining sibling. Mum had told me what to do with her clothes if she died.

Mum's phone ringtone sang thus: "*Tiri murwendo rwekuenda kudenga kumusha kuna Baba*" (We are all on our way to heaven to God the Father). When I told her that that song was very touching, she said, "Don't you know that we have a place to go?" I did not answer, wondering why she was saying such a thing. I assumed it was because we her children lived far away, some of us abroad.

In August, I said to Mum and Sister Phoebe that I was worried about Mum's pattern of sleeping most of the time. They both laughed at me. I then said Mum might be having dementia setting in, so I advised she knit woollen hats and jackets for orphans to keep her mind busy. They both had a big laugh again, but I was worried. In conclusion, they said it was tiredness from heat, work, and walking.

When I came to England, I phoned again to follow up. In August I would not be travelling to Zimbabwe, but my daughter Tariro Julian was going to represent me and my husband at my aunt's daughter's wedding. Mum then said to me that because of family deaths and illnesses, it was worth it for me to return to visit the ill and pay condolences to the concerned family members. I always listened to my mum's advice and suggestions, so I spoke to my family and I flew out just two days before the wedding. Little did I know that I was going to see and hug my mum for the last time.

This breaks my heart and makes me happy as well.

On the day Mum became very ill, Sister Phoebe called me and my brothers, knowing, based on her past experience, that Mum would want that done. Sister Phoebe told me that Mum insisted that she wanted to go to the hospital in the gold three-piece outfit that I had given her in February of that same year. They had to spend a few more minutes looking for it until they found it. She wore it and agreed to go to the hospital. That touches my heart. I have other messages that were left for me which Sister Phoebe told me.

After Mum died, we all got airline tickets and flew from Birmingham and Muyamuri. Michael flew from Manchester. Seven of us met in Dubai, and from there we were in the same plane flying to Zimbabwe. Seven eggs in one basket? I said a *special prayer*, because if by any chance the plane were to have problems, then it would kill my dad to lose all of us. We already wondered how he would manage now that his loving carer (wife) had been given a heavenly birthday. We had a safe flight. God is faithful.

Because of Mum's kind works to the world at large, she was buried in private in the healing chapel which they built after Dad had retired. She knew of this arrangement before she passed away. This was agreed to by

God, the healing committee, supporters, and family. I would like to thank sons-in-law Jacob Matsveru and Davie Baira, and my sister Idi Baira, who helped me clean up the whole house and rearrange the furniture to kick out some memories after Mum's burial, as Dad would have struggled more if this had not been done. Some items were moved out or moved to different rooms. Well done, Sister Phoebe. She was the supervisor.

Missing Our Flight

Dorcas, Jacob, and I were supposed to fly back on the same day, all of us on the same flight. Tsitsi Dorcas's passport had been stolen, so she couldn't go back with us. We were scheduled to be flying back on Monday, but we thought it was meant to be Tuesday; therefore, while others were checking in, Jacob, Tsitsi Dorcas, Izwi, Dad, and I were in the lounge doing paperwork. No one realised the great oversight. Our children thought everything was in order. The next day Jacob and I set off for Harare to board the plane at 10 a.m. Tariro, who was in England, checked with Tinaye to find out what time we would be landing at Birmingham airport, only to be told that we were en route to Harare Airport. On hearing the message from Tinaye, our son, that we had missed our flight, we were devastated, as we had no extra money for new expenses. When I told my aunt Rosemary Bondokoto, she encouraged us not to worry, saying that God and our mum wanted us to look after our dad and comfort him a bit more. All I could say was amen, with a lot of pain and shock though. So we proceeded to see our other aunt, Maria Maruta, who had had a stroke, and then we went to Emirates to sort our new flight dates. We wouldn't be able to fly back until 24 December, which meant nearly another two weeks with our dad. We went back to Gokwe, but because we did not want to hurt our dad, we said we were back because the companies where we worked had extended our compassionate leave. Indeed, Dad still needed our presence and help. There were still things that needed to be put into action, as we later realised. God is a mighty planner. Tsitsi Dorcas, Izwi, Jacob, and I found ourselves in Zimbabwe for more than a month each. However, Jacob and I finally flew back, leaving Izwi and Tsitsi Dorcas to finish up the work of comforting Dad, amongst other things.

—Dorothea Chiwoniso Matsveru

Idi Baira

Mum. I am still trying to come to terms with Mum's sudden departure, or should I call it promotion to glory. I hope this will help me empty out my heart to Mum, Mrs Irene Neddie Muyambi. I would like to take the opportunity to thank my father for setting me up with such a virtuous woman of God as my mother. Also, I would like to give all glory to God the Father for allowing me such an opportunity to be mothered by such a meek and soft-spoken woman who directed her energies into faith and works more than to empty talk. Mum must have been a woman of means to serve humanity as freely as she had without counting the cost.

Mother Teresa said, "Not all of us can do great things. But we can do small things with great love." Mum was a very loving, sacrificial mother who always trusted in God's unfailing mercies. She taught us to love and care for the disadvantaged people in the various areas of life that we find ourselves in. She was such a humble woman of God, always calm and collected in her toils. She never seemed to panic, and always took situations calmly in her own stride.

At home, once a month, we would spend the night in the family lounge, praying and meditating on the Word of God. Mum taught us that prayer is the key to the heavenly treasures.

I do not recall a time when Mum appeared discontented with her surroundings, with her children, or with Dad. She was resolved to devoting her life and time to the work of God and to providing for the needy people she encountered. Mum strongly believed that the chasing of worldliness and riches would never bring her peace. Instead she trusted in the Lord to provide for all her needs and grant her desires per his will.

Mum held us in high esteem and had great faith and belief in us, all her children, but she also managed to release us so we could grow in Christ. Her influence and persuasion was centred around the Lord's will, more than her personal preference for their future. She would pray, "*Kuti vazive zvinhu zvikuru zvavakafanira kutambudzikira mukati mehupenyu hwavo*" (So they may know the most important things that they are supposed to suffer for in their lives).

There is no such thing as the perfect mother, but I can proudly say that our mother was close to the perfect mother, always seeking peace for all. She was and will remain precious to the kingdom of Christ because of her influence on the next generation, and that is our generation as her children and the generation of *vazukuru* (grandchildren) and *vana vevazukuru* (great-grandchildren). Through the power of the Holy Spirit, Mum was a blessing to her children and grandchildren. She always remembered our birthdays and those of our spouses and would call early in the morning to sing "Happy Birthday" to us, regardless of where we were in the world.

Mum actively engaged the Word of God for every problem that she faced at home or at work. She always took time to fast and meditate on the Holy Scriptures regularly, and to speak them and teach them to us. Every morning, we would wake up to a family house prayer preceded by a morning hymn and a Bible reading between 5.30 and 6.00. After that, we would all take turns summarising the passage and saying what we felt the thought of the day should be and what we should learn from the passage. We witnessed her diligence and learnt from her example to apply God's teachings to our everyday lives. My children spent a year with Mum, their grandmother, as a way of bonding with their grandparents. She took great care of them, as if they were her own children. To date, my children always refer to the teachings of Mbuya Muyambi (Granny Muyambi).

Mum always encouraged us to persevere in every situation and to pray persistently.

"You have made known to me the path of life. You will fill me with joy in your presence" (Psalm 16:11). I shall never depart from her teachings.

Mum was a true woman of God. Whenever she was home, we would sense the presence of joy. Her deep-rooted joy sustained her through the difficulties of living with the large extended family that she and Dad had created for themselves. She was an embracing mum who valued the needs of all who encountered her. She was full of wisdom, and never held back advice that would be beneficial to anyone. It's a shame that others were resistant to her words of wisdom, but there were those who accepted her as a loving mum who showed no favourites and no preference of one child over another. She always sought the common good for all. Mum had mastered the ability to encourage us to have joy in the midst of every situation we faced. I remember she would say, "Focus on God, the author and finisher of your life, because that's where you get all your answers."

Family Choir

Mum taught us to sing. It was our favourite pastime in the evenings at home. She would fine-tune our voices to sing different parts that brought harmony to the music. One of her favourite songs features the following lyrics:

> A new command I give unto you, that you love one another
> As I have loved you, that you love one another as I have loved you.
> By this, shall all men know that you are my disciples, if you have love one for another.
> By this shall all men know that you are my disciples,
> If you have love one for another!

I remember when Archbishop Kotso Makhulu visited us in Gokwe to see and bless the works that Mum and Dad were doing. Mum took time every evening to coach us the Tswana versions of the various Mass pieces, like "Obuyitsepo Obuyitsepo Obuyitsepo" / "Unoyera Unoyera Unoyera" ("Holy, Holy, Holy") and "Kwana kwaModimo" / "Hwayana yaMwari" ("Lamb of God").

We would then go on to practise with the rest of the congregation while Mum introduced the songs to the church choir. This always made it much easier for the church choir. Mum used to sing a very strong alto or tenor just to help support other parts, but otherwise she was a natural soprano, hitting all the high notes.

When I was six years old, Mum asked me to read the Bible in church as part of the readings for the service. I had to stand on a stool so that I could reach the lantern. This was similar to the teaching that Mum gave to all her children. She always said, "You should never think you are a guest in the house of God. Wherever you go, let the light of God so shine so that God may be glorified by the radiance of his love that you will be portraying." She would say, "Join in with the music, and participate with the other children of God as if you were just in your mother's house."

Mum was a comforter, not just for the nuns and friars as ordained by the heavens, but even for us children and the community at large. She was a principled woman, a woman of stature who never compromised her beliefs for anything or for anyone. We learnt a lot from her, not just by her teaching us but also mainly by seeing and observing the way that she carried herself.

She was a hard worker who sought to provide for her family, as well as for the extended family around her. She would seek the widows and the orphans and bring them close to her, doing all that she could to provide for them. As a family, yes, we do not hesitate "to rise up and call her blessed", because the favour of the Lord was upon her.

Mum did not want any fuss over her, instead always encouraging us to love our father and the work that God had bestowed upon him. Behind every successful man, there is a strong woman. That is so true for my parents. Mum had her feet on the ground. She was solidly grafted onto Jesus, such that she never allowed anything to move her from her foundation of faith. She never spoke much about herself and was never boastful about her achievements. She was an unsung hero. Many have tried to take credit for the works that she did with her own hands, work that she did for the Muyambi family at large, for the Gokwe community, and for the orphans, nuns, and friars whom she nurtured from a young age.

Mum sowed love, kindness, joy, peace, and unity in all her doings. Another of her favourite sayings was, "Where do fighting and arguments come from amongst you? Do not allow the devil to overcome you in your relationships." Mum knew what it was to have a regenerated heart, and this was the source of her unselfish life and charitable acts. Mum was full of good works. The word *full* refers primarily to her inward grace, which prompted her outward deeds. "Good works are only genuine and Christian when the soul of the performer is imbued with them."

Mum Was a Philanthropist

"I needed clothes and you clothed me" (Matthew 25:36), said Jesus to those who clothed the poor, widows, and needy children. Mum was a woman who mothered the needy, the lonely, and the helpless in the Gokwe community and Zimbabwe at large. The practical unselfish service of this Christian philanthropist has filled the world with fragrance, for there flowed out of that little town of Gokwe a multitude of benevolent and charitable services which are prominent. Internationally there are people who, if they were true to God, would rise up and say, "Mrs Muyambi made me who I am, just by being the person that she was, a woman of few words." It was said by Mother Teresa, "Let no one ever come to you without leaving better and happier. Be the living expression of God's kindness: kindness in your face, kindness in your eyes, kindness in your smile." That describes Mum's way of life.

Mum was mourned and will always be greatly missed. It was a very sad day for the family and the community at large when one of its most beloved and devoted "mothers of many" died amidst her works of charity, finalising the official opening of the Health and Healing Medical Clinic at the Gokwe Centre of Excellence. "Death loves a shining mark, a signal blow," and death certainly found such a mark in the bountiful Irene Neddie Muyambi, whose passing was a blow to the community and the family at large.

Here is a lesson for us all to bear in mind as we part with our saintly philanthropist. Mum was unconscious of the magnificent work she was doing and of its far-reaching consequences. Mum did not seek to sit in high places. She did not aspire to be a leader, but was content to stay in her own home and try to do all she could in all the ways she could.

Sudden death can fall upon any of us. I say this not to make anyone fearful, but simply because it's true! Mum was ill and grew worse—and she died within a space of hours. It was a bitter blow for all of us whose lives had been positively affected by the gracefulness of Mum. We always ask, why did she died?

The Lord permitted it for some wise and loving purpose. We still cannot explain why suffering, accidents, sickness, and death afflict us, but God knows what he is doing, and one day we shall understand. Sickness, suffering, trials—these are meant to be channels of grace and power for God's glory to be revealed.

If a person is a faithful servant unto others, if she is righteous and generous, it does not mean that she will be spared the tribulations and trials of life. We can only imagine how Mum became tired in performing her endless errands of mercy and her deeds of kindness, rising at five o'clock in the morning, taking care of her husband and her mum's needs, teaching and heading the nursery school, performing administrative work around the whole Muyambi complex, and then holding devotions in the evening until she probably could do nothing but topple into bed, totally exhausted. Such tiredness grows from day to day and finally takes its toll.

Mum's homecoming was a triumph for her, as her labours were acknowledged in the presence of the Lord Jesus. But for us it was a heartbreak, which only God the Holy Spirit can handle! Speak tenderly; let there be kindness in your face, in your eyes, in your smile, in the warmth of your greeting. Always have a cheerful smile. Don't give only your care, but give also your heart.

Sweet mother, I'll never forget you, for the sufferings you suffered for me.

Lawrence Muyambi

This is just a glimpse of how I really feel and what Mum's love means to me. I saw her beauty and grace through her expressions of faith; I learnt her strength when I should have folded. She mapped the way to heaven and above by showing me the utmost kindness and more love than I could ever ask of anyone. I caused her some grief and gave her reasons to worry and be concerned. I messed up along the way, but she loved me despite and because of all that. I saw a reflection of God in her face. Her love knew no bounds; it was a love that knew no end, a love that never judged or questioned. I'm so glad she chose to be all of this and more to me. With that being said, I thank you, Mum, for all you have done for me. You will always be the best mother there could be. Until we meet again …

Tariro Matsveru

Grandma was a gentle woman, gracious and full of love. She was always on the go, going to the school where she worked, going to conferences where she would teach other women, and joining in celebrations and mourning with those who mourned, up until the last time I saw her, three months before her passing. And little did I know that it would be the last time.

Though I live here in the United Kingdom, Grandma always made sure she reached out if I ever went for a period without getting in touch. She would ask about what I was doing and where I was going with my life, and emphasise prayer throughout the conversation. She always wanted to be in the loop. She always made birthdays—my birthday!—feel extra special, because every year, early in the morning, she would ring just to sing "Happy Birthday", even if others would forget. Her small yet big show of love would make my day. This was something I wasn't ready to go through last year without, as my birthday came a month after her passing.

Through her many acts, she taught me faith. She taught me to trust in God and gave me the knowledge that the Bible should be one's best friend. She showed me that you can never have too much love or give too much. I learnt to be a shoulder to lean on for others, to be trustworthy, and to be accountable. She showed me the beauty in forgiving and laughing. And now, it's not the same without her around, without her singing, "*Tarira mufaro wandinawo*" (Look at the joy in my heart), without having the little phone calls to catch up, or ask her what she wanted when from the United Kingdom when I was coming home to Africa, or to ask her to tell Granddad that I was ringing him and he was not answering his phone. I believe she is in a better place. She fought a good fight, and now my angel is up there in heaven resting. I say, "Rest well until we meet again. I will treasure the memories, the advice, the laughter, and the good times, and I will miss you. Here is to forever loving you."

Be at peace ...

Conclusion

"Let us drink tea; death has come into the world" was Neddie's saying which meant that we need to make hay when the sun still shines. Let us do what we must do, with the knowledge that one day we will die and depart from this world. Let us eat and drink when our throats can still swallow, because one day it will be in vain.

Prayer, fasting, forgiveness, peacefulness, helping the sick and suffering, and helping the needy materially, financially, spiritually, and psychologically was Neddie's life. So was building accommodations for the sick, orphans, students, and nuns, and growing fruits and vegetables to share with everyone who passed by, including strangers.

Neddie never missed church services. She never heard of a death and ignored it or heard of an illness and failed to visit to offer prayers.

Her battle was with the devil, not people.

Her husband was her priority; she made sure he was all right before she went anywhere. Neddie had high respect for Lazarus. She loved him and educated her children to respect their father. She was a unifier of not only her family but everyone. Neddie chose peace over instability. She disassociated herself from hate and divisive talk. She was not the type of woman who could die a silent death; her deeds follow and live after her. She shall be remembered forever and ever.

Neddie is a name derived from Neddie of Eardweard. It is of English origin, and means "guardian of wealth"; "one who leaves no loose ends"; "one who gives advice to help, not to please"; "one who will be a friend forever"; "one who repairs, rebuilds, and creates"; "one who never wavers from the truth"; "one who does not waste energy on needless worry".

A truly good woman, Neddie was someone in whom you could put your trust.

In this book I have tried in some way to enlighten readers, to illustrate the life history of Irene Neddie and her husband, Reverend Lazarus. The inseparable couple (until death did them part) worked tirelessly together for the good of everyone.

This book has highlighted how Irene Neddie fell seriously ill and eventually died from traumatic pain. The seven stations of her journey towards death were observed by those around her. The wise words she shared with all who came into contact with her are recorded herein.

This book has also tried to answer questions of why events went the way they did after the death of this virtuous woman, why Lazarus and Neddie were frustrated so much by the people they had helped and worked with over the years.

In this volume, we looked at the history of CZM, a religious community which Lazarus and Neddie had founded and owned. The diocese would not offer any help to build the community, but they did advise that my parents start this independent community which should sustain itself. The couple went on to start this community, keeping nuns in their own house.

This book has tried to make it clear to all why Neddie deserved a chapel burial. She was special and unique. What is good, is good. Neddie deserved the best. Her contribution to the Mothers' Union (MU) must not go unmentioned. For over fifty years she worked in the MU, a charitable organisation within the Church of England. She recruited hundreds of people to join this organisation that supports families in times of sorrow and happiness.

The book has also answered questions about what position the Diocese of Central Zimbabwe took in regard to Neddie's burial. Neddie looked after orphans, blind people, sick people, and the homeless. She looked after deaf and dumb people, lepers, people with learning disabilities, and those with epileptic fits. She was a woman who cared for the crippled, the barren, those who were mentally ill, the suffering, the needy, those who had been widowed. She was a woman who built a convent, a monastery, an orphanage, a clinic, the Healing Centre, a primary school, and a girls' high school. She was a woman who died in the process of applying for land to build a boys' high school and a university. She died asking for her title deeds for the land she was sure she had worked for without diocesan financial support. It was a struggle that compromised her own family.

Although she is dead, Neddie's work speaketh.

Gone but never forgotten.
May her soul rest in eternal peace.

Sources

Ackroyd, Peter, *Shakespeare: The Biography* (New York, 2006).

"Burials", National Churches Trust, http://www.national churchestrust.org/what-see-outside/burials, accessed Dec. 2016.

Chivaura, Vimbai Gukwe,(a) "The Relationship between Ancestors and the Living in Shona Culture", 21 May 2015, *The Patriot*, https://www.thepatriot.co.zw/old_posts/the-relationship-between-ancestors-and-the-living-in-shona-culture/, accessed 21 Nov. 2017.

Chivaura, V.G. "The Shona Worship God directly, Not through Ancestors", 14 May 2015, *The Patriot*, https://www.thepatriot.co.zw/old_posts/the-shona-worship-god-directly-not-through-ancestors/, accessed 21 Nov. 2017.

"Christ Church, Zanzibar", Wikipedia (last modified 11 Sept. 2017), https://en.wikipedia.org/wiki/Christ_Church,_Zanzibar, accessed 10 Oct. 2017.

"Famous People Buried in Winchester Cathedral", Ranker, https://www.ranker.com/list/famous-people-buried-in-winchester-cathedral/reference, accessed 10 Oct. 2017.

Fawcett, Jane, *Historic Floors* (Abingdon, 2007).

Godricson, Godric, "The Burial Customs of the Ancient Greeks", God's Acre (1 Oct. 2015), http://godsacre.blogspot.com/2015/09/the-burial-customs-of-ancient-greeks.html, accessed 21 Nov. 2017

Jongwe, T. D., *Christian Healing Mission in Gokwe, Zimbabwe: A Success Story* (Xlibris. New York, 2017).

Heritage Inspired, http://www.heritageinspired.org.uk/index, accessed 23 Nov. 2017.

"Known Graves of Holders of the Victoria Cross in Zimbabwe", VictoriaCross.org, http://www.victoriacross.org.uk/ggzimbab.htm, accessed Dec. 2016.

"Leadership and Governance", Church of England, https://www. churchofengland.org/about-us/structure/churchlawlegis/canons. aspx, accessed Dec. 2016.

Mothers' Union Handbook, Diocese of Birmingham.

"National War Memorial", OttawaKiosk.com, http://www.ottawakiosk. com/national_war_memorial.html, accessed 21 Apr. 2015.

Stephens, Charles, *The Jurisprudence of Lord Denning: A Study in Legal History*, i: *Fiat Justitia: Lord Denning and the Common Law* (Cambridge, 2009).

"The Tomb of the Unknown Warrior", British Legion, http:// branches.britishlegion.org.uk/branches/shipston/remembrance/ the-tomb-of-the-unknown-warrior/, accessed 23 Nov. 2017.

Lightning Source UK Ltd.
Milton Keynes UK
UKOW01f0201270218
318536UK00001B/27/P

9 781543 487275